Birnie Bairn

A Morayshire Childhood

1944-1957

Margaret Jeary

ISBN:1482065169
ISBN-13:9781482065169

Dedication

For my children Lynn and Iain, grandchildren Catriona, Euan, Hannah and Heather, Mum and Dad who are now 90 and 97, my sister Rosie who shared my childhood, my brother Allan and sister Jayne who were born after we left Morayshire and my husband Peter who knew so little of my childhood.

Acknowledgements

Memory is a fickle thing and I could not have written this book without help from Mum and Dad and especially from my sister Rosie who recalled so much that I had forgotten. I would like to thank my husband Peter and friends Jacqui, Sue and Wendy for their advice and support, also Lynn and John for their IT expertise.

CONTENTS

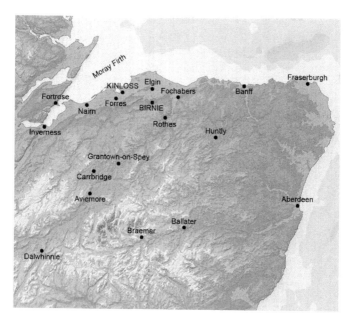

North East Scotland - My Childhood World

(derived from map of Scotland by Eric Gaba licensed under CCSA)

Author's note

Life has changed so much since the nineteen forties and fifties when Britain was recovering from a second world war. Attitudes and morals have changed and there have been huge advances in medicine and technology which, as a child, I would not have believed. I can remember living in my grandparents' cottage and seeing farmers using cart horses yet ten years later I flew in an aeroplane; something I would never have dreamed of. My grandparents, born in 1888 and 1890, lived to see men reach the moon.

Encouraged by my children, I wanted to write down my memories before they were all forgotten. I have tried to explain to the present generation how different life was in those days.

The village where I was born is called Thomshill on maps but it was always referred to as Birnie, the name of the parish.

I have written everything as accurately as I can remember and I apologise for any mistakes.

I have been careful not to identify anybody other than family who may still be alive as they may not wish to be recognised.

1 MY ARRIVAL

I was born in a thunderstorm at 2.10am on June 2nd 1944 in my grandparents' house, the Smiddy Cottage in Birnie, near Elgin in Morayshire. I was delivered by Nurse Williams, the District Nurse, who lived in the cottage next door with her cocker spaniel Rufus. At the time my father Allan Bartrop was in the Royal Air Force and stationed at Bogs of Main (known as RAF Elgin) but he was at Birnie for my arrival.

Me aged one

I cannot remember anything about the Smiddy but I'm told it had a stone flagged kitchen floor and when I was a baby I didn't crawl, I scuttled along on my hands and feet with by bottom in the air because the floor was cold and rough. Sometime during my childhood, the cottage and the ruined blacksmith's workshop next door were demolished and council houses were built on the site. This would have been in the early 1950s.

Glenlossie Distillery dominated the village which also had a community hall and a grocery shop. A couple of miles away there was a very old church, Birnie Kirk, which my Granny often walked to on a Sunday evening and where my ancestors are buried. The church, where Mum and Dad were married and my younger sister Rosie and I were christened, was built in 1140 and was the first cathedral of the Bishops of Moray.

Birnie Kirk

Most men in the village, like my grandfather James Kerr, worked at the distillery. Next to it was the distillery farm where he had worked during the war, when production of whisky was closed down because the fields were needed to grow crops for food.

The distillery had its own cooperage where casks were made and the barley for the whisky was spread out on the floors of large warehouses and regularly turned by men using large shovels. This was called 'malting', to encourage the barley to sprout and create sugars. Those jobs would have been labour intensive and nowadays most distilleries buy in casks and malted barley from elsewhere. There was also a resident excise man, called 'the gauger', who lived in a fine house owned by the distillery. There used to be a row of lovely flowering chestnut trees between the road and the buildings but sadly they have all gone.

Mum was walking along this road one day with my Rosie who was a baby in the pram and I was sitting on the apron. There were no safety harnesses in those days and I fell off, banging my head on the road and creating a small bald patch which is still there. Rushing off to A &E was unheard of and we just went home. I expect I howled all the way.

In my first year, we moved from the Smiddy to Distillery House at the other side of the village. This would have been when the distillery reopened after the war. My grandfather worked as a stillman and he only had to walk across the back yard then climb into the distillery through a window. His job had an interesting perk because before leaving the distillery at the end of the working day, every day, he and the other workers received a free tot of whisky. Grandad used to carry a metal whisky tot in his pocket which had an old penny for a base and rings of copper coloured metal which could be pulled away from the penny to form a drinking vessel, then squeezed flat like a concertina. It used to fascinate me and I wish I knew what happened to it.

It was here that my sister Rosie was born on December 16th 1945 and we lived here while Dad was in stationed in Palestine. We didn't go to Palestine because of the troubles there; families were not allowed to go. We were finally reunited when Dad was posted to RAF Kinloss in 1948 and we moved into a married quarter there a few months later.

Glenlossie Distillery

Distillery House had originally been a two –up and two - down cottage, probably built when the distillery opened in 1856, but at some time a kitchen and scullery had been built on to the back so that a tiny room in the original house had a window looking into the scullery. That small room was where Granny and Grandad slept and there was only space for a bed, a chest of drawers and a kist, a chest which opened at the top. There was no heating but it was surrounded by other rooms so probably didn't become too cold. Upstairs there were two bedrooms and a box room. Granny's lodger had one bedroom and the box room and the other room, which only had a bed, was used mainly for storage and laying out apples to keep them fresh. There was usually a bucket of eggs, dipped in isinglass to preserve them. Among the odds and ends stored in the room was a gas mask which hadn't been thrown away after the war. One day, I thought I would put it on so I pulled it over my face then discovered that there was a large moth flapping about inside it. I couldn't get the mask off fast enough!

When Rosie and I slept in one of the bedrooms downstairs a fire would occasionally be lit if it was cold. Granny had two hot water bottles; one was dome shaped and made of copper and the other one was referred to as the 'stone' bottle. They would probably be collectors' items now. Clothes were stored in chests of drawers; there were no wardrobes but at the time I didn't think that was strange because I had never seen a wardrobe. The mattresses and pillows were full of feathers, occasionally needing a good shake.

There were wartime black roller blinds on the windows which were still pulled down at night and the curtains were made of white net, not fabric. The walls were papered. Mum was the decorator and she had to cut the edges off the wallpaper before pasting it on to the walls. Granny had a few pictures hanging in the bedrooms, including a sombre nun with the words 'Abide With Me'. My favourite was a little girl tempting a kitten to play with a piece of paper dangling on a string. Grandad had been in Egypt in the First World War and brought home a present for Granny, a pair of black velvet cushion covers colourfully embroidered with the stag's head badge of the Seaforth Highlanders. Across the bottom were the words, 'To my dear wife from Kerr'. The embroiderer had made a mistake as Grandad's name was James! I doubt if Granny had ever owned anything so exotic and they were never used, they were put in frames and hung on the wall. They still hang in my mother's house.

The scullery was a small room off the kitchen with a sink which only had a cold tap and draining board. The water came directly from Glenlatterach reservoir but when Granny was a little girl the water where she lived came from a stream which ran past their house. One day she and her mother went for a walk along the stream and they found a dead sheep lying in it. This was their drinking water!

Hanging on the scullery wall was a set of stag's antlers mounted on wood and Grandad used to hang his tweed bonnet on the points.

Later a bathroom was built on to the scullery but it looked nothing like the bathrooms we are used to nowadays because it was simply a room with a stone floor, a roll top bath, a wash basin and green hot water tank which stood in a corner. Before the bathroom was built there was a water closet just outside the back door next to the coal shed, but a new toilet was installed in the bathroom. The water in the tank was heated from the kitchen fire in winter but seldom in summer and water for washing ourselves and washing dishes came from the kettle. It always sat on the kitchen range where Granny did all her cooking, even after electricity arrived about 1948. I remember her baking scones and oatcakes, always wearing a floral wrap-around apron and her slippers which she called 'moggans'.

After retirement, my grandparents moved to an old cottage near Fochabers which had only two electric sockets, no hot water system, no bath and no cooker. Granny, born Margaret Mary Gordon Mathieson in 1888 at The Wards in

Elgin, chose to cook on an open range until her death in 1976.

The house had been built on sloping land and at the back of the bathroom, which was lit only by a skylight, there was a retaining wall and the land above the wall was the back garden. Up there, Granny grew blackcurrants, gooseberries and rhubarb. She kept hens up there too; there was a henhouse and a large hen run. We always had fresh eggs when the hens were laying and, as a rare treat, one was occasionally killed for the pot if its egg-laying days were over. Granny would put the hen on the ground, put a broom handle over its neck, stand on it and the hen expired. It was plucked outside then gutted, creating an awful smell. She then poured some methylated spirits on to a metal tray, lit it and held the plucked hen over the flames to burn of any remaining bits of feather. The smell of that was worse that the gutting. Hens (nobody referred to a hen as 'chicken' in those days!) were never roasted, always boiled with vegetables in a big pan on an open fire. There was an oven in the range which could bake milk puddings but it was probably not hot enough for roasting.

When Granny wanted more hens, she would set eggs under a 'clockin' hen', one that wanted to sit on eggs. She only wanted female hens and to 'sex' them she took each egg and held a dangling needle on a thread above it. The needle either swung from side to side or round and round; one way was male and the other female but I can't remember which was which. Then the broody hen was given the female eggs to sit on. You may scoff but it seemed to work!

The washing line was in the top garden and to reach it Granny had to carry everything up wooden steps with no handrail. Behind the top garden, creating a lot of shade, was a big black shed which was one of the distillery peat stores. There was another huge outdoor peat stack near the farm. All this peat was needed for the furnaces used for distilling whisky.

*****

2 PANDROPS AND CLOOTIE RUGS

The kitchen was very gloomy because the only window looked on to the side of a whisky warehouse which must have been built after the cottage, taking away the light and the view. Granny used to wipe the windows with a rag dipped in DDT, now banned, and the flies died instantly. Sticky fly papers also hung in the kitchen and scullery. There was an open range where all the cooking was done, a table and four chairs, two old armchairs and a couch. My grandfather's army kilt from the First World War had been carefully unpicked to make a long length of tartan which was spread over the couch like a rug. In one corner was a built-in cupboard which Granny always referred to as 'the press' and it was many years later I discovered that it was the Gaelic word for cupboard, although neither she nor Grandad spoke Gaelic. There was a large polished wood wireless set run from a battery which Grandad occasionally took into the distillery to charge up. The only other piece of furniture was a dresser where the crockery was kept. A few ornaments sat on the shelves, including a Staffordshire flat back of a man in a kilt with a sheep which Mum found on the village rubbish dump when she was playing there as a child. It was black with soot but she took it home and now it sits in my china cabinet. There was a blue plastic box with a lid which always contained pandrops, Granny's favourite sweets. They were round mints and I have the box now, a memory of my childhood. In the dresser drawer they kept their ration books.

The floor was covered in linoleum and several 'clootie rugs' made from strips of woollen cloth pulled through a sugar sack using a gadget called a cleek. Everything was re-used and recycled so all woollen garments were kept and cut into strips about half an inch wide. A wooden frame was kept in the shed and it would be hauled out when a rug was to be made. Sugar sacks were then stretched across the frame and tacked into place then, using the cleek, the strips of cloth would be pulled through the sacking in loops. Usually the rugs were random stripes but my mother made scenes of thatched cottages with colourful gardens and usually a lady wearing a bonnet, a long dress and holding a basket of flowers. Mum's best rug in this style was made for a Daily Express competition in 1947, the first in a national newspaper after the war. At the last minute she was short of a strip of navy blue to finish it and ended up being given a pair of navy blue school knickers by a neighbour, just the right shade of blue. She won second prize and received £5, a tidy sum then. The rug was displayed in a shop window in London then it hung like a tapestry in its polished wooden frame on the sitting room wall at our house in Kinloss. She still has the rug.

Before electricity came, the room was lit by a Tilley lamp which sat on the kitchen table and we carried small paraffin lamps to bed. I cannot recall ever seeing candles. The kitchen range was always lit and sometimes the fires in the bedrooms were lit, but not very often. As well as Granny's little bedroom, two rooms on the ground floor had double beds. The one opening off the kitchen would have been the 'front room' but Granny had no need for such a nicety as the kitchen had a couch and two armchairs as well as the table and chairs.

When my great-uncle, Grandad's brother Philip, became very ill he came to live with us and he was attended by Nurse Williams. I remember her washing her hands at a bowl in the bedroom; this was before the bathroom was installed. He died, but I must have been very young because that made no impact on me. Many years later, my mother made a family tree and discovered that her Uncle Philip, who was apparently a gentle soul, had been in prison for ten days after being in a fight. Mum couldn't believe it. Uncle Philip had said that after he died, he was to be taken back to his home in Elgin and laid out there so that his friends could come to see him, as was the custom in those days.

Mum with one of her rugs.

Outside the back gate was the woodpile, called the hag stack. All tree branches dragged from the nearby wood and every other bit of wood they found was propped up against the retaining wall next to the wooden steps to dry out, then it was sawn up on a saw horse to be used as firewood. Granny and Grandad often did this job together, one at each end of a long woodman's saw. There was some coal in the coal shed but the main fuel was wood or peat. If Granny wanted a really hot fire to make scones on a girdle she threw fir cones on to the fire, creating a huge blaze.

There was a tiny garage, built by Granny's lodger for his motor bike. It only needed one wall, a roof and doors as the

Mum, Dad, Rosie and me sitting on the saw horse with the distillery peat shed at the back.

back of it was the retaining wall and the other side was the wash house. As the roof was about the same level as the top garden, Rosie and I used spend hours playing 'houses' on the roof. There was no thought of 'health and safety'! We used to make mud biscuits in the lids of cocoa tins and bake them in an oven made from bricks with a slate roof which became hot in the sun. We actually tasted them and of course they were horrible!

Granny did her 'big wash' in the washhouse, which had a
boiler heated by a fire beneath it. After the sheets and
towels were boiled (tablecloths were never used, the kitchen
table was covered in a piece of wipe-clean oilcloth) they were
rinsed in the sink in cold water, put through the wringer and
laid out to dry in the sun on a piece of grass near the distillery
building. Smaller items were washed with blocks of green
soap in a tin tub and rubbed on a washboard to remove dirt,
then hung on the washing line.

The washhouse was where they stored their bicycles. Granny
had a 'sit up and beg' style of bike and she cycled to the
village shop and sometimes to Elgin. As well as going for the
milk every evening, on Sundays Grandad used to cycle to
Fogwatt, on the road from Elgin to Rothes.

It used to be the law that if you wanted to buy a drink on a
Sunday you had to be a bona fide traveller and travel at least
three miles. At Fogwatt there was a house with a shop in the
front room which sold beer and Grandad went there to buy a
drink. I suspect Granny disapproved because after they
moved to the house which they bought after Grandad retired,
he used to hide a bottle of whisky in the washhouse and go
there, out of Granny's sight, to have a dram. When my Mum
and Dad visited them, Dad used to join Grandad for a drink in
the washhouse.

After his travels in the First World War, when he was in
France and Egypt, I doubt if Grandad ever went further than
Elgin but my Granny decided to go and visit her sister in
Londonderry. On the boat, a young man gave up his bunk so
that she could lie down instead of sitting on a seat all night.
Her oldest sister Helen had married Charles Crossan who was
a cattle dealer and she probably met him in Elgin because the

Mathiesons, Granny's family, were also cattle dealers. Her brother Ernest used to cut meat at 3a.m. for the town butchers and he owned the land where the Eight Acres Hotel in Elgin is now situated. I was too young to know much about the Irish trip but while she was there she sent a letter to Mum which had smudged ink, caused by tears. I was never told why. She brought back shamrock brooches for Rosie and me and they were always kept in a drawer at our house in Kinloss, because if we wore them we would lose them. I don't know what happened to them in the end but we never did get to wear them and to this day I occasionally bring the subject up with Mum!

Granny had another sister called Penuel, named after a place name in the Bible, who emigrated to Canada in the nineteen twenties. Every week, Granny posted the local paper, the 'Northern Scot,' to Canada and as letters were expensive to post, the news would be written on the page margins and the paper was then tied up with string. That was a cheaper rate of postage. Penuel used to send us her local newspaper which had pages of comics with characters like Blondie and Dagwood. We used to look forward to reading them because they were so much more interesting than the 'Northern Scot'.

*****

3 GRANDAD THE HERO

What I didn't know until I had grown up was that Grandad had saved Glenlossie Distillery from burning down. On March 12th 1929, a fire broke out and it was Grandad who found it.

He was one of three staff on the night shift when the power failed. He found that the dynamo room was on fire and started to put it out with a hand held hose but the fire had already caught hold. His two colleagues, David Mutch and James Miller, ran to the village to raise the alarm while Grandad continued trying to put out the flames. People ran to nearby farms to find more men to fight the fire and within half an hour the distillery's steam fire engine was working.

According to the report in the local paper the 'Northern Scot,' flames shot to a hundred feet high and two roofs collapsed. The men, including Grandad, climbed on to the roof with hoses but couldn't stop the fire spreading to the malt tower and from there it would reach the drying lofts and barns which contained up to 20,000 quarts of barley. The fire engine at Rothes was summoned and rushed eight miles to Glenlossie. The newspaper said that the malt tower contained 1,000 bushels of malt and became a furnace when it was not possible to get water into the building. The manager, James Marshall, had a gun and fired shots, breaking the roof window then the men were able to reach the blazing malt. When the fire engine arrived, the fire was brought under control. According to James Miller, the night maltman, 'The hero of the outbreak is undoubtedly James Kerr. His early efforts in the blazing dynamo room gave us a chance to summon help in time and he stuck to his job with the main hose from start to finish.'

The report concludes by saying that the distillery was owned by the Distillers Company Limited and was one of the largest malt distilleries in the world.

The headlines were 'Distillery Blaze Hero' and 'Workman Fights Great Fire Alone'. That was my Grandad, but he never spoke about it.

During the nineteen fifties, a film was made about whisky distilling at Glenlossie and Grandad featured in it. Eventually, we all went to the village hall to see the film and there was Grandad, walking round a whisky warehouse, holding up a lantern to read the dates on the casks. There is also a book about Scottish whisky distilleries and in the chapter about Glenlossie there is a photo of some men rolling casks. One of them is Grandad.

When he retired he was presented with two Parker Knoll armchairs which sat in their front room and were never used. I still have them.

The house had no lawn as the front garden was also cultivated. There was an apple tree in the centre and Grandad kept a few hives of bees by the warehouse wall, protected from the wind. One day, when he was trying to listen to the news and I was making a noise, he told me to 'go away out and count the bees'. So off I went, with my golliwog Geordie. Nobody was offended by golliwogs in those days and I loved him! I soon realised that there were more bees inside the hive than outside so I found a stick and started to poke the entrance. I was quickly surrounded by angry bees and ran off screaming, 'Save Geordie! Save Geordie!'

When sugar was rationed, much of Granny's precious supply

was put aside to feed the bees in the winter and we did
without sugar on our porridge and in our tea so that the bees
could be fed.

Grandad in 1973

Apart from a few flowers by the front door, which was never
used because everybody came and went by the back door,
Grandad used the front garden to grow peas, potatoes,
onions, carrots, beetroot and cabbages. Granny and I used to
squash the cabbage white butterfly caterpillars which ate the

leaves because there were no pesticides. Broccoli was unheard of and there was no need to grow swedes because they grew in nearby fields. He also grew a few lettuces which Granny used to make lettuce sandwiches and in the days of sweet rationing it was a treat to have a small, new lettuce leaf filled with sugar then eaten like a sweetie. Another sweet treat was a slice of bread and butter sprinkled with sugar. Sweets didn't 'come off the ration' until 1953 but we didn't feel deprived because what we had never had we didn't miss.

Over the front garden fence were the roofs of whisky storage warehouses which were like huge Nissan huts in shape, side by side and joined in a row. Because of the sloping land, the garden looked down on these roofs, which were coated in tar. One day, Granny and Grandad were sitting in the garden when, unexpectedly, one of the roofs collapsed, making a huge noise and clouds of dust. That didn't stop us from continuing to run over the other roofs, jumping from one to the other because it was a short cut to another part of the distillery.

In the nineteen fifties, we could sit in Granny's garden in the summer and hear the raucous calls of corncrakes in the field between the house and the village. Mrs. MacPherson who lived in the village was given a dead corncrake to look at because they are shy birds and seldom seen. It was lying in her porch when a visitor called and she picked it up to take it to the door when the bird suddenly revived and flew away! There are no corncrakes on the mainland now; the few left are confined to the Western Isles.

Outside the back door was a small yard with the outside toilet, complete with a supply of newspapers. Yes, we really did wipe our bottoms with newspaper. Next to the toilet was the coal shed which was also used to hang dead rabbits, hares and pheasants. Granny chopped logs into sticks there and on one occasion she cut her thumb quite badly. She was taken to Dr. Gray's Hospital in Elgin and was kept in as the poison went up her arm. We went to visit her in the hospital; it was Christmas and she had been given a little doll as a present from the nurses. In the other corner by the coal shed, high on the wall and in the shade there was a meat safe. This was a cupboard with mesh sides to keep food cool and the flies off in the days before homes had refridgerators. At the other side of this yard was a wooden gate and I can remember standing there looking out into the area between the house and the distillery and seeing deep snow, far too deep to go out and walk through. That was the terrible winter of early 1947 when I would have been three.

Beside the wash house was the rubbish pit, called the midden or ashpit, where everything that couldn't be composted or burnt was thrown. Once in a while a man would come with a horse and cart to empty it. Near the washhouse was a large boultry (elderberry) bush which would be laden with sprays of black berries in the summer but Granny didn't do anything with them, such as making jelly or wine. She didn't drink alcohol but once when my mother was young Granny made ginger beer which fermented in the bottles. They all exploded.

My Granny's grandmother Jane Duncan lived a few miles away at Blairn Hall near Glenlatterach, in the days when illicit whisky was made at home and kept out of sight of the 'authorities'. One day, she walked to Elgin with a jug of whisky to sell and as she walked along the street she was

Playing by the River Lossie

spotted by an excise man who told her to follow him. She was still carrying the jug when a friend who was standing in a doorway saw her, so the friend held out her apron, Jane dropped the jug into it and walked on. Without the evidence, there was nothing the excise man could do!

*****

4 PORRIDGE AND PANCAKES

The garden and the hens supplied a lot of the food we ate. Grandad also had a fishing rod and snares so we had trout and salmon from time to time as well as rabbits. One day Grandad asked my sister Rosie and me to go and check his snares along a nearby fence. Well, we found a rabbit in a snare, still alive and struggling to escape. We felt very sorry for it and couldn't get the tight wire off its neck to let it go, so we unwound the snare from the fence wire and carried the rabbit home to Grandad. Oh how innocent we were. The rabbit was quickly dispatched and hung up in the coal shed! Granny's lodger had a shotgun so we also had a supply of hares, pheasants, duck and pigeons. Before myxamatosis arrived in the early nineteen fifties, we ate a lot of rabbit. It was good, cheap meat and there was a local man who caught rabbits to sell. He had them strung from his bicycle handles and he even looked like a rabbit. With hindsight we ate rather well, all fresh organic food, but at the time I thought we must be poor because the butcher's van only came once a week.

Every morning, Granny made a pan of porridge for breakfast. The porridge oats came in a hessian sack which she bought from a mill in Elgin and she brought it home balanced on the handlebars of her bike. The sack was stored in the pantry. The porridge was made by boiling the oats with water and salt and after it was cooked, full cream milk was poured over it. Grandad ate his plateful about nine o'clock and by then he had done an hour and a half at work on an empty stomach.

In the evenings, in all weathers, Grandad cycled to a farm called The Level and collected his pail of milk, identified with coloured plastic rings on the handle. It was still warm from the evening milking and would not have been pasteurised as it had come straight from the cow. Sometimes Rosie and I walked with him and she remembers drinking some of the warm, creamy milk out of the pail lid on the way home. We tried to avoid the bubbly jocks (turkeys) which seemed huge to us and they would chase us. Cash was left in the empty pail to pay for the milk and the change would be left in the bottom of the pail, then the milk was poured over it. Granny soon put a stop to that!

Lunch, every day except Sundays, was cooked in one big pot on the open fire. In the pot was a piece of meat and various vegetables, with the addition of barley for broth or sometimes peas or lentils. She often made potato soup as potatoes were plentiful. The soup was served in wide soup plates, far larger than modern soup bowls, then the meat and vegetables followed in the same plate. Potatoes were always boiled, in a separate pan, never roasted. Then there would be a milk pudding or stewed fruit, or for an occasional treat Granny made a rich, fruity cloutie dumpling which was placed in a bowl, covered with greaseproof paper then boiled in a big pan of water. It was like Christmas pudding but without the alcohol and it was delicious when eaten hot.

Granny had a day off from cooking once a week so on Sundays lunch was 'tatties and milk'. Potatoes such as Kerr's Pinks from the garden were boiled, mashed and some creamy milk added. We always drank tea as coffee was an unheard-of luxury. We had coffee after we moved to Kinloss, either Camp coffee which was actually coffee and chicory essence and had a strange flavour, or Nescafe powdered instant coffee which came in tiny 2oz tins. The government supplied tins of National Dried Milk for youngsters and also bottles of concentrated, unsweetened orange juice which we drank diluted with water.

Girdle scones were made on the open fire and milk which had been left to stand in the pantry until it curdled was added to the flour mixture. The scone was cooked on a girdle in a flat, round shape then divided into four wedges and eaten with butter and home-made jam. Every summer, Granny made enough jam to last a whole year. Fruit and sugar were boiled up in a large copper jam pan. She had no jam thermometer to tell her when setting point was reached, nor did she bother with a smear of jam cooling on a saucer to see if it wrinkled when it was touched. She knew the right moment because 'It speaks to you', she always said. Then it was put into jam jars, some so old they were made of pottery, a circle of waxed paper was put over the surface of the jam then it was covered with a lid of newspaper held in place with string. She made raspberry, gooseberry, blackcurrant, rhubarb, bramble and sometimes strawberry jam, which Rosie and I called 'run away mile' jam because it *was* runny and difficult to set. Brambles (blackberries) were always made into jelly. The fruit was boiled then strained through a jelly bag, suspended between two chairs in the front porch where it could drain undisturbed. The filled jars were stored in rows on shelves in the cupboard under the stairs. Rosie and I helped Granny with the fruit picking and we were jokingly told to whistle all the time then she would know we weren't eating the blackcurrants.

At the farm where Grandad went for the milk there was an area of waste land covered in raspberry bushes. Granny used to go there to pick the berries for jam and one day, it would have been in the school holidays after we moved to Kinloss,

Rosie and I were there helping her. There was a sudden thunderstorm and we sheltered under the bushes from the heavy rain. I was wearing a red blazer and as it became soaking wet, the red dye ran out in rivulets all over me. Wild raspberries are usually red but sometimes bushes of yellow ones can be found. One year Mum made yellow raspberry jam but it turned out such a disgusting shade of brown when it was cooked that nobody would eat it.

Rosie and I had never heard of fruits such as oranges, pineapples and bananas which were unobtainable because of the war, at least in Birnie. When Mum first showed me a banana she said, 'What's this?' and I replied, 'a fish!'

When we had fish, Granny used to say, 'It surely is an awful crime, to fry the back afore the wime' meaning that you fried the stomach side first. I expect the fish came from a fish van but she could remember when a woman walked from Lossiemouth to Birnie, over nine miles, to sell fish from a barrel on her back.

As well as girdle scones she often made drop scones, which we called pancakes, and oatcakes which we ate with butter and golden syrup. After cooking the oatcakes on the girdle, they were propped up on irons in front of the fire to dry off and this made them curl slightly.

To iron clothes, Granny heated several flat irons in front of the fire and ironed everything on a thick layer of pieces of blanket, topped with a sheet, on the kitchen table. She acquired an electric iron when the house was wired for electricity and used it until it exploded with a bang and a flash. She got such a fright that she went back to using her old flat irons. These were the ones which were propped in front of the fire to dry out the oatcakes.

We didn't own a toaster, even at Kinloss, and toast was made by putting a thick slice of bread on to a long handled toasting fork and holding it in front of the fire until it browned then turning it over to brown the other side. This took a while and your face and hands were toasted too but I swear it was

Granny in her garden.

tastier than from a toaster. It was even better with a spoonful of honey from Grandad's bees; there was always a honeycomb in the kitchen dresser. We didn't know that honey could be bought in jars.

Granny and Grandad were quite self sufficient, keeping hens, growing fruit and vegetables and living off the land but some things had to be bought in. As well as the butcher's van there was also a weekly Lipton's van selling groceries. The village had a small shop, run by 'Shoppie George'. Flour, pieces of cheese cut off a whole cheese with a wire cutter, lentils, barley and butter as well as Granny's pandrops were bought at the shop. The garden in front of the shop had a slatted fence and one day Rosie's knee became stuck in the slats. It wouldn't come out and began to swell. Shoppie George came out with some butter which he smeared all over her knee and eventually it slid out, swollen and painful.

Anything that the shop didn't stock such as hardware, knitting wool and dress material had to be bought in Elgin. Granny used to knit socks on sets of four needles made from wire. Grandad could knit too because the wire needles came from his time in the army in France during the First World War when he knitted his own socks.

As the bus only came twice a week, a trip to Elgin often involved a cycle ride or a four mile walk. In January, Granny would cycle eight miles to Elgin and back to buy Seville oranges to make marmalade. She went in all weathers and I don't think she owned an umbrella.

*****

5 VESTS AND THE VELVET DRESS

The only heating in the house was open fires and the kitchen was always warm because the fire in the range was on most of the time. I cannot recall feeling cold at that house even though the bedroom fires were seldom lit and the scullery and bathroom had no heating at all. Later, we moved to Kinloss and that was a cold house!

I suppose we dressed to keep warm, always in natural materials as there were no man-made fibres in those days. I've heard of women making underwear and wedding dresses from parachutes but none came our way. In cold weather I wore a vest and on top of that was a garment called a liberty bodice which buttoned down the front with rubber buttons because they didn't break in the wringer. Jumpers were made of pure wool and would have been knitted by Mum, as were the knee-length fawn coloured socks. Knitted hats were called pixie hats and I see from old photos that I was well wrapped up.

Mum made a lot of our clothes but once a year she and Granny went by bus to Aberlour where there was a well-known orphanage which held a huge jumble sale called 'Japp's Sale'. I was never taken on these trips but Mum would come home with clothes for us, including one garment I've never forgotten, a white, all-in-one sleep suit with a buttoned flap over my bottom in case I needed to go to the toilet in the night. Oh, the shame of it!

Mum bought me a pretty pink velvet party dress at the sale. It had puff sleeves and smocking on the front and I would have worn it to a Christmas party for RAF children at Kinloss. I also wore it for the class photo when I was in primary three.

Eventually I was allowed to play in it. Then, on holiday at
Birnie, I was climbing about in a tractor when I got it covered
in black oil and that was the end of the pink velvet dress.
Later, Mum made me a lovely cream taffeta party dress
covered in net and I wore it to a Christmas party. I don't know
what happened to it in the end but I was certainly

Wrapped up for the cold in 1948

never allowed to play in it. Little did I know that it was the
last 'posh frock' I would own until my wedding day!

As well as dressmaking, Mum could play the piano and violin and she could paint and draw. In the days before printed colouring books, she would draw elephants standing upright and wearing dresses and Rosie and I would colour them with crayons.

During wartime rationing, when Mum wanted to give a wedding present of some china, she and a friend each bought a few plain white cups, saucers and plates with their coupons to make a set of six and she painted a spray of blue flowers on each one to make them less 'utility'. They had to make do and mend in those post war times.

*****

6 STRAWBERRIES AND SCARLET FEVER

Distillery Cottage was even older than Distillery House, a one-storey cottage where my great-grandfather George Kerr lived when he was head of the distillery. This was the home of Robbie, Alec and Neil, the three boys we played with. Their parents cultivated a strawberry bed in their garden. One summer holiday Rosie and I woke very early and decided to get dressed and go outside, even though nobody else was up. It must have been about six o'clock.We wandered near the boys' cottage and saw the strawberry bed, full of luscious red berries. The temptation was too much and we climbed over the fence and helped ourselves, assuming that nobody would be around to see us. We *were* seen, by a workman in the distillery; word got back to Grandad and we got a good telling off.

Scarlet fever seems to be a thing of the past now but it was a serious illness when I was young and one day I saw Robbie taken away in an ambulance, wrapped in a blanket. Contagious diseases were treated in isolation hospitals or 'fever hospitals'. Luckily he recovered.

We also played with Isobel and Cameron who had a yellow Labrador called Rex and they had a swing as well as large rhododendron bushes to climb in and play hide and seek.

There were families at the distillery farm cottages and one little girl who lived there, called Dottie, was a 'blue baby', a condition which was untreatable then. We used to play together but sadly she died when she was five, after we had moved to Kinloss.

One day there was a violent thunderstorm and for some

reason there was nobody in the house but me. I was very frightened so I ran to the farm cottages where Dottie's mother let me sit by the fire until it was over. She had just baked a chocolate pudding and oh, I wanted to taste it but I wasn't offered any. There was nothing so exotic in Granny's kitchen.

The daughter of another family there became pregnant when she was single, a disgrace which was talked about in hushed tones in those days of strict morals. I remember going to see her arriving back from her wedding and I was expecting to see her in a white dress and veil, just like my bride doll. I was disappointed because she wore a long yellow dress and didn't have a veil. I once asked Granny if she had a wedding dress and she told me she was married 'in blue'. I thought this meant a blue wedding dress but it turned out to be her best blue suit, the normal wedding clothes for ladies like Granny. Mum and Dad were married during the war and as there were no coupons for a wedding dress; they and their bridesmaid and best man wore their RAF uniforms.

Mum used to visit a friend called Mrs Coutts in the village and she had two daughters, Ruby and Jacqueline. She used to take us to visit them and we would have tea and nice things to eat, like biscuits. Granny didn't have biscuits.

Apart from the neighbours, the only visitor I can recall was my cousin Jim. Mum's older sister, my Auntie Peg, lived in Woking where my Uncle Charlie had gone to work in an aircraft factory. They had two children, my cousins Jim and Carol. In the summer, when he was a teenager, Jim used to cycle all the way from Woking, up the A1 and through Scotland to visit his Granny. You couldn't do a journey like that on the main roads now!

I started school at Birnie Primary in the summer of 1948. I would have been four in June so I was very young and of course there was no nursery or playschool in those days and no preparation at all for this big change in my life. Mum arrived home from Elgin with a new schoolbag for me and I was taken to school and left; that was it. Up until then I had only played with Rosie or, very occasionally, with Dottie, or Jacqueline and Ruby. Before I went to school I had limited contact with other children and none at all with boys (Robbie, Alec and Neil came to live next door later) and when I arrived at the school I was put to sit at a double desk next to a boy – an alien species! I burst into tears.

Marriage of my parents Allan Bartrop and Isabel Kerr in 1943

The school was only a ten minute walk from our house, unlike Granny's school which was a four mile walk and she had to carry her lunch and a peat for the fire. Birnie school was small with only two classrooms. The toilets were outside, with no hot water for hand washing. The headmaster, always referred to as 'the dominie', was called Mr. Morrison and he taught the older pupils while Miss Burns taught the younger ones.

In Granny's garden 1952

Mr. Morrison lived in the schoolhouse which had a large garden at the back and many apple trees. The garden could be accessed from the field behind it, out of sight of the house, so we used to climb over the fence and fill our pockets with apples. I don't know why we bothered because they were horrible and sour. Years later, my father told me that Mr. Morrison's son was lost in a plane crash over Italy in the war and as Dad was in the RAF, Mr. Morrison always asked if anything had been heard about his son. He was never found.

The autumn half-term holidays were always called the 'tattie holidays' because children used to help pick the potato crop. Before mechanisation, this was done by hand and everybody who was able turned out to help. No doubt the bit of extra money was welcome. I used to take Granny's 'piece' to the field. This would have been something like bread and cheese in a brown paper bag and a flask of tea. The flask was a Thermos but instead of a plastic screw-on cap the stopper was made from cork and pushed into the opening. It would have had a bit of greaseproof paper wrapped round the cork to help prevent the tea from leaking out.

The school took part in a Christmas concert in the village hall. We all had to stand in a row on the stage and sing but I don't know what we sang because I didn't know the words and remember being bewildered by it all. The dress I was wearing was dark brown wool with long sleeves and buttons at the cuffs, obviously one of Mum's home-mades, cut from some adult garment. This was just after the war, when everything was scarce. Standing next to me was Miss Mustard (I can't remember her first name, I was only four) and she was wearing a pretty pink net party dress. To me, she looked like a fairy princess. And there I stood in my drab brown dress. I've never forgotten the humiliation!

However, we were well off compared to some because we had a home, clothes and food.

Apart from the school concert and my tears on the first day, I cannot remember anything about Birnie School as I was only there a short time before we moved to Kinloss.

*****

7 THE PLANE CRASH

Monday, July 5th 1948 was a lovely, sunny summer day and
Mum was going to take me and Rosie, who was in a
pushchair, for a walk. However, there was a delay as Mum
and Granny stood chatting to a neighbour. Impatient to go on
the walk, I set off on my own and it was then that I saw a
sight I have never forgotten; I watched an aeroplane tumbling
out of the sky, turning over and over as it fell. Then it
disappeared out of my sight behind the distillery buildings.

Mum and the man she had been talking to also saw the plane
falling and set off running to where it landed, on a farm called
Easterton. When they arrived, they found the plane and the
pilot in flames. Mercifully, he would have died on impact.
Mum was only twenty five when she witnessed this horrific
sight.

RAF Kinloss and what was then RNAS Lossiemouth are in
Morayshire so I frequently saw aeroplanes and knew that
they were little things that flew in the sky like birds, but as I
was only just four I had no concept of their real size and that
there was a man inside. I had no concept of distance either,
because I thought the plane had fallen behind the distillery
and I can remember for a long time afterwards running round
that building to visit my friend Dottie, holding my hands
tightly on my head in case another plane fell out of the sky
and hit me.

For some time afterwards, there was a bare patch in the
barley field caused by the fire and a piece of the aeroplane
lay propped against the fence. One day, Mum was walking
along the road near Easterton when a car pulled up and a

lady got out and asked her where the plane had crashed. It was the pilot's mother, who had come to see where her son had died. Mum showed the lady the area but of course didn't mention what she had seen that day.

When I was older, I was told that two planes from Lossiemouth had collided and for the rest of my life I wondered about the crash and the pilot. When it became possible years later to search on the internet, I discovered that the planes which collided were Seafires from the Fleet Air Arm based at Lossiemouth. Seafires were the naval version of Spitfires, with folding wings for storage on aircraft carriers. They were practising formation flying when the accident occurred and the collision destroyed the cockpit of one plane, causing it to crash and killing the pilot, Francis Joseph Curtis. He was a Probationary Pilot and he was only twenty one and single. He was the son of Francis Curtis, a hotel timekeeper and his wife Angela and they lived in Liverpool, where Francis was born in West Derby on 16th April 1927.

The pilot of the other plane was Petty Officer Raymond Walker R.N. and he survived. Although his cockpit was damaged, he managed to bail out and landed near Glenlatterach Reservoir, breaking his ankle as he landed. Luckily some Girl Guides were camping nearby and they ran to help. They bound his ankle and carried him on a stretcher to their camp, where he was collected in an ambulance. Francis Curtis is buried in Anfield Cemetery, Liverpool. In 2011, I visited the grave and left flowers. At last I felt at peace with the terrible memory of his death.

*****

8 PLAYING IN THE DAYS BEFORE TELEVISION

The farm at the distillery was a great playground for us and our friends, Isobel and Cameron and the three brothers, Robbie, Alec and Neil. When we lived at Kinloss we spent holidays and most weekends at Birnie where we used to roam the fields and play in the farm buildings. The farm had two huge Clydesdale horses which pulled carts and ploughs; this was before tractors were commonplace. Rosie can remember being lifted on to the back of one of the horses and being very impressed. When I visited Birnie in 2012, the old farm buildings where we played had gone and only the cottages were left.

The farm grew barley for the whisky but they also had cattle which were called 'stoats' or 'stirks', young males kept for beef. They attracted biting insects called clegs, horrible things, and when Rosie was bitten on the calf of her leg it swelled to twice the size. I walked with her to the other side of the village where Nurse Williams lived and she put ointment and a bandage on the bite. The path to the River Lossie, another favourite playground, passed through a field of stirks and one day, crossing the field with Rex the dog, the cattle decided to chase us. Running with all these beasts thundering after us was a frightening experience which I've never forgotten and I have kept well out of fields of cattle ever since. Luckily we all made it to the fence before they caught up with us.

Another time we were out with the dog, his foot became trapped in a gin trap, legal in those days, which was hidden in sand at a rabbit warren. This was before myxomatosis when rabbits were plentiful and caught for the pot. In the distance we could see a man ploughing a field, so we ran to him for help as our hands weren't strong enough to pull the trap apart. Rex survived but we kept away from rabbit warrens after that.

We spent most of our time playing outside as there was nothing much to do indoors.

We used to lie on the grass looking for four leaved clovers (we did find them!) and making daisy chains. We would pick a buttercup and hold it under somebody's chin; if their skin glowed yellow, and it always did, it proved they liked butter. We went for long walks, eating fruit when we found it, like wild strawberries, raspberries and brambles. I remember being with Grandad somewhere beside the River Lossie, reaching up to pick huge brambles which Granny would have used to make jelly.

We would go to the nearest field of 'neeps' and choose one each, hold it by the leaves and bash it over a fence post so that the root part came off, then eat it raw. What a treat that was! 'Neep' is the Scottish word for turnip but, confusingly, they were actually swedes.

We chewed the sour leaves of sorrel, which we called 'sookie sourocks', and played at 'sodgers' (soldiers) with long stems of plantain. You would pick a stem and hit your opponent's stem, taking it in turns, until the plantain head came off. The countryside was beautiful because wild flowers grew everywhere, especially along the road verges. We had lords and ladies, purple fumitory, red and white clover, blue speedwell and lady's smock. Farming practices have changed a lot since the nineteen fifties and we no longer have the flocks of peewits (lapwings) which were commonplace then. Local councils cut the grass verges along roads now but on Shetland you can still see all the wild flowers I remember from my childhood. When I went there it was wonderful to see them all.

The garden of the distillery manager's house, which was originally built for my great-grandfather but he refused to live in it, had a large area of mature rhododendron bushes with branches which you could sit on and bounce up and down, playing at 'horses'. We rode side saddle of course and the best branches had names like Merrylegs, from the book 'Black Beauty'. The bushes were also great for playing hide and seek.

That house was where I first saw a television set. It would have been about 1956 when TV reached Morayshire and it was only in black and white and had one channel, the BBC.

The River Lossie afforded hours of fun. We didn't swim in it, mainly because we didn't own anything as fancy as swimsuits and couldn't swim anyway. We didn't even venture in to paddle as the water was always cold, although I know we paddled there when we were small, supervised by Granny, because a photo exists of us paddling with our dresses tucked into our knickers. One day Rosie and I found a pool full of eels. We ran home for a tin bath from the washhouse and filled it with water and eels. It had a handle at each end and between us we carefully carried it home. Granny was unimpressed and the eels ended up in the distillery burn.

Every summer Mum made us new, matching dresses for the school prize giving and when I was twelve we also had hand knitted boleros. Rosie's was fluffy pink angora and mine was plain pink. I was very put out because I didn't have an angora bolero too. Anyway, that summer holiday we were allowed to wear the boleros out to play and Rosie was wearing hers

Playing at the River Lossie 1947

when we went to the river. She was crawling along a branch over a deep pool when the branch broke and she fell in. The lovely angora bolero was a dripping wet mess. I'm ashamed to say I thought it was funny!

Rosie's memory of this is not quite the same. Here is her version:

"I remember falling into the pool. I was lying out on a thick, dead branch when it broke and I fell into water, over my head. There were lots of tiny fish darting away and I walked up the slope of the pool to get out. No-one came to help me, I could have drowned. I don't remember the pink bolero, I thought I was wearing a red dress with polka dots. When I got home I took it off in the bathroom and tried to dry it on the hot water tank so I didn't get into trouble. I don't know now if the trouble was for falling in the river, getting my dress wet, or both."

A favourite pastime at the farm, besides hide and seek, was climbing about in the store of straw bales which were rectangular in shape and good for building. We used to make long tunnels then crawl through them and it never crossed our minds that the bales could collapse and smother us.

Near Granny's house there was a large tree at the top of a steep bank. Somebody had tied a length of rope to a branch and we used to grab the rope and swing out over the chasm below. If the rope had broken or we'd let go we would have been injured but nobody gave that a thought. That game stopped when Granny asked Grandad to take the rope down before we killed ourselves. The tree, with its smooth bark, was covered with carved initials as pen knives were carried like toys in those days.

The distillery had three small dams, fed from a burn. The first dam was small and became silted up. Occasionally the dams were drained and Rosie and I saw trout dying from lack of air in a small pool of water. I waded out on to the silt to catch the fish, sinking into it as I went. I had no idea that I could have sunk into the sand forever. I couldn't reach the fish so we ran home to find some planks which we laid on the wet sand and I crawled over them. The trout were duly lifted out and taken home where Granny fried them for us. I don't think we told her how we had caught them! Nowadays the dams are surrounded with fencing to keep everybody out.

When I think back to the places where we played, the trees we climbed and other potentially dangerous things we did as we roamed the countryside unsupervised I'm amazed we all survived childhood. We weren't wrapped in cotton wool like children today.

Before we went to school, we each had a tricycle. These would have been recycled from somewhere as we didn't have anything new, probably because such things weren't available after the war, and mine was painted dark green.

I had my golliwog called Geordie and Rosie had a teddy called Teddin which had green knitted shorts and a green and brown checked jumper. On a car trip along a remote country road she was holding him out of the car window and of course she dropped him. It was some time before we convinced Dad to turn and drive back for miles until he was found. Teddin was thrown away with a lot of our belongings when we packed up to go to Singapore in 1957 which upset Rosie at the time but she has a teddy now!

When we had to stay inside, we had to find ways to amuse ourselves. There was no TV and we didn't listen to the radio until we moved to Kinloss as Grandad only listened to the news. We made scrapbooks using pictures cut from magazines and Granny made glue by mixing flour and water to make a paste. She also showed us how to play Snap, a simple card game, and we helped with the baking and jam making, usually 'topping and tailing' gooseberries. Covering a comb with a bit of paper and blowing though it made 'music' of a sort. To tell the truth there wasn't much to do indoors, that's why we preferred to be out in the countryside.

Eventually, a milk delivery started to come to the village for those who didn't want to cycle to the farm and we used to help the girl driver in the summer holidays. It was a small van with two doors at the back. We used to sit in the open doorway with our legs swinging over the edge and when we reached each house we would jump out and leave the bottles of milk. Can you imagine that being allowed today?

Both Mum and Granny belonged to the Birnie branch of the Scottish Women's Rural Institute. When I was about three, they had a coach trip to Lossiemouth, the nearest seaside town. Children could go too, so off we went and I very nearly didn't make it home. Lossiemouth had huge concrete blocks on the beach, to prevent enemy craft landing I believe. Some are still there. Well, I saw people jumping off these blocks into the sea and I thought I would like to do that. I managed to get myself up on to a block and jump off, not realising that you needed to be wearing a swimsuit and, more importantly, be able to swim. Luckily, somebody hauled me out but I was soaked to the skin. I have never been allowed to forget it!

Another outing I'd prefer to forget was when Granny took me to Elgin by bus. Waiting in a queue to come home, a bus pulled up in front of me and I climbed on board. Other people followed, but not Granny. I screamed because I was on the wrong bus and the laughing passengers let me off. I blame that incident for my dislike of public transport; I feel anxious thinking all the time that I'm on the wrong bus or train.

Christmas was a non-event in my grandparent's house, it was

just another day. There were no cards, no decorations, no tree, no special meal. After 1948, Rosie and I spent Christmas at Kinloss with Mum and Dad and we each had a stocking, of the hand-knitted up-to-the-knee variety which we wore to school, tied to the end of the bed with a safety pin. In the morning we would find games and an orange and apple and a sixpence. I can't recall sweets of any kind as they were rationed until 1953.

The one Christmas I do recall at Birnie, it must have been before 1948 when we moved to Kinloss, Rosie and I each received a beautiful doll dressed as a bride. Everything was scarce after the war but Mum had bought two dolls and she added hair to their bald heads by dyeing curly lambs' wool, then she made the dresses and veils. We woke on Christmas morning to find them sitting by our beds, propped up on Granny's flat irons. I was thrilled.

At Kinloss we had a floor-to-ceiling tree taken from some nearby plantation. It was covered in decorations which included my Dad's Mickey Mouse tree toys which his uncle gave him about 1926 and I still have them. We had paper chains on the ceiling, Christmas cards and I've no doubt we had one of Granny's hens for lunch. When we lived at R.A.F. Scampton in 1961 the postman came on Christmas Day (yes, people worked, Christmas wasn't the big holiday then as it is now!) carrying a very soggy brown paper parcel and inside was an oven-ready hen from Granny.

Mum could make and ice cakes and when we were young we always had one on our birthdays but I can't remember a Christmas cake or pudding. However, we weren't at all deprived, we were just like everybody else.

After Christmas Day, we were taken the fourteen miles to Birnie to spend the rest of the holiday with Granny. Kinloss, as a playground, was pretty boring and we much preferred being at Granny's house as there was so much more to do. Granny's lodger was always a source of entertainment and presents.

*****

9 CATAPULTS AND CARS

Like Grandad, Simon Ross worked in the distillery. This was just after the war and there was no daily transport to and from Elgin and nowhere to stay except to lodge with someone. He had a bedroom and box room upstairs and he ate all his meals with the family. He had the use of the bathroom but used to shower at the distillery which provided hot showers for the workers.

Playing on Simon's motor bike 1948.

He was the driver of the little steam train which travelled along a track from Glenlossie to Langmorn Station a couple of miles away, taking draff (the leftovers from the barley, used as cattle feed) and whisky to the main railway line. It was he who built the garage for his motor bike and Rosie and I often travelled on the pillion going to and from Kinloss (separately!) without crash helmets. I think he had a leather helmet. Eventually, he bought a black Morris Minor, number BCT 407, with a fold- down hood. One day he was driving too fast over a hump back bridge and the car left the road, bounced and both doors flew open, bounced again and the doors slammed shut. We thought that was hilarious.

Cars didn't have seat belts in those days. Once I was travelling in the back of a car, sitting next to the door. Mum was beside me with Rosie on her knee. I was fiddling with the door handle and Mum told me to stop, which I did, so Rosie promptly leant over and touched the handle. I knocked her hand away, the door flew open and I landed on the road. Mum thought I was dead, until she heard me howling. Luckily my only injuries were two scraped knees.

Eventually, Dad bought a car, a black Morris 8, registration GWA 848. Rosie and I would have been about seven or eight and we were staying at Granny's when he and Mum arrived in the car. We both thought it was a taxi and couldn't believe it was ours! Dad was a member of the Automobile Association and our car had a yellow AA badge on the front. AA patrol men, who travelled on motor bikes, always saluted us and Morris 8 drivers would wave to each other.

Simon occasionally took us to the cinema in Elgin to see films like 'Moby Dick' and 'The River of No Return'. One Saturday, he wanted to stay on in Elgin so after the film he sent us home in a taxi. It was early on a summer evening and just outside Elgin we saw a strange little cloud, pink from the setting sun and shaped like a child's drawing of a cloud. A white trail, like an aeroplane's contrail, came out from one side of it and although the driver stopped and we watched it for a while, no aeroplane appeared. The driver told us that he and his passengers had watched exactly the same thing the previous evening. It was very strange and I have often wondered what we were looking at.

In the days when there were not many toys about, Simon used to make things for us, like a train made from a National Dried Milk tin and bits of wood, painted green, which we could pull along on a string and he also made us a doll's crib. We had bows and arrows and he made us stilts. We became quite adept at walking about on them. Rosie and I also had a wooden cart which she sat in and I pulled along. He taught us how to light fires with a magnifying glass. He was also the source of catapults, which children are not allowed to have these days and no wonder. The distillery had skylight windows and we used to fire stones into the sky and wait for the tinkle of broken glass. Eventually the workmen realised how the skylights were being broken and there was a big row. Yes, I do feel ashamed.

Rosie and me with our cart.

He used to tell us stories, often about his wartime experiences in Italy when he was in the Lovat Scouts, and he bought magazines full of pictures called 'Illustrated' and 'Picture Post'. This was in the days before television reached

Morayshire, so seeing all these pictures, some in colour, was a novelty.

He would take us out each Easter Sunday to roll Easter eggs, which were just hard boiled eggs. Nobody had chocolate eggs because sugar and sweets were rationed. People used to dye the egg shells with tea or coloured rags but Granny didn't need to because she had some black hens, called Aurocana but she would not have known that, which laid blue and green eggs. We would take the eggs with bread and butter in a brown paper bag to somewhere with a grassy bank and roll them down until the shells broke, then we sat and ate them. One Easter, it was snowing so we went to the nearby wood and Simon built a shelter from branches, then we sat inside it to eat our eggs. Such simple pleasures and far removed from the chocolate extravaganzas of today!

After Simon bought the car, he would drive to Elgin on Sunday mornings for a newspaper, taking us along if we were staying at Birnie. We would stop at a milk bar with a juke box and have a huge ice cream with ice cream soda each. What a treat that was!

Occasionally he bought us fish and chips or perhaps a local delicacy, mealy jimmy and chips. A mealy jimmy is a white pudding, like a sausage, filled with oatmeal, bread and usually mutton fat, dipped in batter and deep fried. We also had mutton pies made with hot water pastry which are referred to as Scotch pies nowadays and made with lamb. They were all very fattening but we didn't care, they were tasty! The chip shop in Elgin had tiled walls and on one wall was a large picture, made with tiles, of the old bridge at Craigellachie. The chip shop has long gone and I expect the picture was destroyed.

Every Christmas, he hung up a stocking for each of us by the bedroom fireplace so we had a second lot of presents to open. He was in the Territorial Army and every summer he went to a training camp for two weeks. I suppose it was a free holiday for him, as one destination was Towyn in Wales. He always brought presents back for us, like buckets and spades and beach balls. One year, he brought home a brooch for me, a 'cameo' with the Queen's head on it and a 'gold' ballet dancer for Rosie. In class one day, a girl showed the teacher a brooch she'd found, *my* brooch! I told the teacher it was mine and she looked disbelieving but the girl had found it on a path near our house and there was a hole in the bottom of my schoolbag. Finally, I said that Rosie could tell her it was mine; only then was I allowed to keep it. I still have it in my jewellery box.

People ate what they could find, by fishing or poaching, and to vary our limited post-war diet Simon used to take us egg collecting. He would climb trees to take pigeons' eggs which were always plentiful. So were peewits, so common in those days you had to be careful not to step on their nests if you walked across a field of grass. We only ever took one egg from a nest as the bird would lay again. Oyster catchers used to lay their eggs in shallow scrapes on the shingle by the River Lossie and sometimes we went to find gulls' eggs on a heather covered hill called the Buniach. We used to test them for freshness by placing each egg into a pool of water. If they stood upright they were fresh and if they lay horizontally they would be put back into the nest. Then we would take a few eggs home, boil them in a pan on the open fire and eat them with a pinch of salt.

Simon had a gun and shot pigeons, ducks and hares. In the

holidays, he would take us with him in the distillery train when it went to Langmorn Station. He would let us slow the train by winding a handle, then shoot at pheasants in the fields. 'Health and Safety' would be horrified. On the way to Langmorn, the train had to stop at a level crossing and we would get out to open the gates, holding on as they swung across to close off the road then back across the railway line. One day, Rosie must have been hanging on near the top of the gate and as it clanged shut, she shot over the top on to the line. A lump the size of an egg appeared on her forehead but she survived, howling all the way home. She still has a slight lump on her forehead.

I must have been very young when we were with Simon in a friend's house at Pluscarden and we were looking at an animal lying on the kitchen floor. He told me it was a wolf! It was a roe deer and I have no idea if he or somebody else shot it but I expect we were all grateful to have something different to eat. We were told not to mention venison to anybody, it was a big secret and the deer's innards were buried under the apple tree in Granny's front garden.

As well as his shotgun, he had an army pistol which would have been brought back from the war. One day he, Rosie and I were sitting outside and he had the gun. We were allowed to fire it and the bullet I fired hit the wooden frame of a distillery window. I wonder if it's still there?

Granny came out to see what was going on but we all looked innocent. Many years later, he took the gun to Lossiemouth and threw it into the harbour. Another souvenir of the war was a German officer's hat which I used to wear 'dressing up' and Rosie wore his Lovat Scouts beret.

For a short while Simon had a cocker spaniel called Judy, much to our delight. Granny made him keep the dog in the garage, then he had to rehome her to his friends at Pluscarden. Rosie says that Granny made him get rid of Judy because of the messes she made in the back yard. I don't think she ever had a four-legged pet until we went to Singapore in 1957, when our cat Whisky went to stay at Birnie and she lived there to a ripe old age. However, Granny did have a canary called Joey and later a green budgie called Jocky which could speak.

Dressing up.

Grandad, born in Knockando in1890, was well over retirement age when he finally stopped work in 1963. He was kept on because the distillery was short of men. They had to leave Distillery House because it was a tied house and move away, so they bought a cottage at a place called Clochan, near Fochabers where they lived until Grandad died in 1974 and Granny in 1976. They are buried in Elgin cemetery.

When I went to look for Distillery House in the nineteen nineties it had been demolished, so both the homes of my early childhood have gone.

Life moves on.

*****

10 NEW HOME, NEW SCHOOL

At the end of 1948 Dad returned from Palestine and was posted to RAF Kinloss, so Rosie and I were uprooted from the home we knew. It was only fourteen miles away from Birnie but to us it was another world. Mum, Rosie and I made the journey by train from Elgin to Kinloss railway station and I had my green tricycle with me which I rode from the station to our new home. Dad had been given a semi-detached house, 4 Married Quarters, which was newly built of pebble-dashed brick and had metal window frames. When more houses were built the roads were given names and we became 13, Tedder Road. The new roads were given the names of Air Marshalls such as Tedder, Salmond, Trenchard, Portal and Harris.

The small kitchen, divided from the dining room by a cupboard unit, was heated by a small coke stove. There was an electric cooker but no fridge because people like us didn't have fridges. In hot weather our bottles of milk stood in a bucket of cold water out in the back yard. At first, Mum did all the washing by hand in the sink but later they bought a washing machine which cost £25.

There was a sitting room with a coal fire, which was useful for roasting chestnuts, and the window was what we called 'French doors'. We'd call them patio doors nowadays. Upstairs there were two bedrooms, a large one with two metal hospital beds which were so high that Rosie and I could barely struggle into them and a smaller room next door with a double bed. There was a bathroom and a separate toilet. Once a week, on Sunday evening, Rosie and I had a bath. Dad filled it for us and I still remind him that those baths were far too hot! He forgot we were children! The rest of the week, we had what was called 'an up and down wash' with Palmolive soap and a flannel and every day we cleaned our teeth with Gibbs toothpaste which came in a small, flat, blue metal tin. The paste was pink and we rubbed our wet toothbrushes on it to create foam then brushed our teeth.

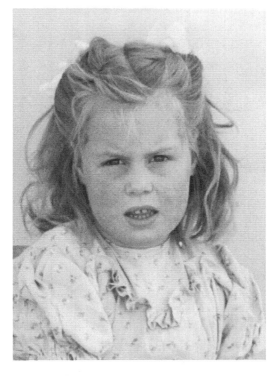

In 1949, my first school photo.

Each bedroom was heated by a small, wall mounted electric fire. Someone had advised Mum that they were expensive to run so they were almost never used. Rosie and I slept in the larger room at first, then our beds were squeezed into the smaller room. No reason was given at the time but I was eventually told by Mum, when I was fifteen, that the house was haunted, especially in the large bedroom.

Outside was a small yard with a coal shed and we had an equally small back garden with a washing line. Later we were given coal bunkers for the coke and coal and the coal shed was used to store things like bicycles and the lawn mower. This was before the Morris 8 appeared and Dad used to cycle to work on a yellow RAF bike, the style intended for ladies. He had to take what was available at the time.

Mum cooked traditional 'meat and two veg' dishes but we also had Scottish delicacies like skirlie, which was oatmeal and onions fried in dripping (this was long before we cooked in olive oil!) and bubble and squeak which was fried, leftover cooked cabbage and potatoes. We also had a tasty dish called stuffed skirt of beef. The skirt was a long piece of meat with a membrane on one side. This was pulled back to make a pocket which was filled with oatmeal and onion stuffing then it was sewn up. Mum pot roasted it with onions until it was tender and delicious. You never see skirt of beef in butchers' shops nowadays.

We also had toast, cooked under the grill of the cooker, spread with beef dripping and sprinkled with salt. We had never heard of calories and cholesterol.

Mum used to bring gorgonzola cheese home from Lipton's shop in Elgin. When Rosie was learning to speak she called it 'goglonzogla' and one day, to her embarrassment, Mum found herself in Lipton's asking for 'goglonzogla'.

We had never heard of pizzas, fish fingers, broccoli, yoghurt, avocado pears, kiwi fruit and all the other 'foreign' produce we take for granted today. Herbs were mint for peas and parsley for white sauce and we certainly didn't use garlic. We only had ice cream when a van came round selling tubs, cones and wafers. Flake bars hadn't been invented and the most sophisticated ice cream the van sold was called cherry pie which was just a little tub of vanilla ice cream with glace cherries in it, eaten with a small wooden spatula. Another van which came round once a week sold fish and chips. We could buy a little bag of chips for threepence, just over one new penny today.

Our school photos 1951

Kinloss Primary School was on the road to Findhorn and I went to school there. I had a beret with the KPS badge on it and a purple and green school tie. There was no uniform and I wore a kilt for most of the year and cotton dresses in the summer. A gabardine coat kept out the wind and rain. During my childhood and teens I always thought I didn't have enough clothes but I have tried to make up for it since.

At first Rosie and I walked to school along the main road, or paid a penny for the bus if it was raining, but eventually a cinder path was built inside the fence which separated the road from the RAF station. It seemed a long walk to the school and back and in winter and even with sheepskin boots and fur gloves our feet were so numb with cold that when we arrived home Mum used to let us thaw them out in a basin of warm water. The walk was made worse because some days we were tormented by Shackletons and Lancasters doing 'circuits and bumps', practising taking off and landing. We could see them coming in over Findhorn Bay, getting lower and lower then roaring over our heads to land on the runway. 'There's an aeroplane coming! Run!' It was quite frightening and no matter how fast we ran we couldn't escape them.

The old part of the school had two classrooms and a canteen but as the RAF camp expanded a prefab with two classrooms was added. The walls were thin, the floor was cold concrete and the heating in each classroom was a coke stove with a guard round it. My memory of school in those rooms, one for the primary fives, the other for the primary sixes and sevens, was of being cold and having cold feet all the time. The unheated toilet block was outside, with flush toilets but no washbasins. They were in the main building; there was no hot water and the towel was a cotton roller towel, permanently cold and wet. It's hard to believe how primitive things were then and, by modern standards, unhygienic. Eventually, another block of classrooms was built for the little ones which had indoor toilets and washbasins.

We sat in twos at old wooden desks which were stained with ink from the ink wells in each corner. We had pens with nibs which we dipped in the ink to write then used blotting paper to soak up the excess ink. We had a pencil each and the teacher would slice a sliver of wood off the end and we had to write our name on the exposed wood. The pencils were handed out in the morning and collected again at the end of the day.

We were weighed and measured once a year and we had visits from the 'nit nurse'. We were taken out of class one at a time and the nurse looked through our hair. As far as I know, nobody had nits and I was in my sixties before I ever saw one.

At first we stayed at school for school dinners as it was such a long walk home. The food was cooked at Forres Academy canteen and delivered to Kinloss in metal containers. Irish stew, which was a dollop of meat, potato and carrot, was a favourite and we had milk puddings you never see nowadays like sago, tapioca and semolina as well as rice pudding with a spoonful of jam on top. We ate in the canteen on long tables for eight but we didn't have chairs, we sat on long benches.

We were given free school milk by the government, probably to supplement a poor diet after the war. The bottles, a third of a pint in each, were glass and when I was in the third year there, a boy swallowed a broken piece of glass from the rim and was taken off to hospital. The crates of bottles were delivered to the school and on freezing cold mornings the milk would expand and push the cardboard tops off. The milk would be full of ice crystals and put to sit by the coke stove to thaw out. Then on hot summer days, the milk would be 'off' by morning playtime when we were given it but most days it was drinkable, with a thick layer of cream at the top and I liked it. If we were thirsty (no drink was provided at lunchtime) there was a water fountain outside the school building. Of course in winter it froze. On one occasion the Australian government gave schoolchildren a box of six tins of fruit each and I recall struggling home with the box, which became heavier with every step.

Primary 3 at Kinloss (centre middle row in my velvet dress)

During the morning interval we had our milk then we were sent outside, in all weathers. If it was raining we had to shelter in the bike shed but if it was fine we used to play games. Hopscotch was always popular and so was skipping. Throwing a ball against a wall and catching it was another game and we progressed to using two balls, like juggling. There were games called 'What's the time Mr. Wolf?' and 'The King of the Barbarees'. Marbles were sometimes the current fad and we girls used to dance to the song 'She wears red feathers and a hula hula skirt'. I must have been a hilarious sight, hula dancing in my kilt!

It was at Kinloss Primary that I first sewed and knitted. I made a basic lap bag, like an apron with a large pocket at the front. I've never seen or used one since. Then the girls had to make a pair of cotton knickers with elastic round the waist and legs.

The problem was the size. There was only one fit-all pattern and although I completed mine, they were too small and all my time and effort was wasted. I must have been able to sew reasonably well because I made a bib and embroidered it with flowers for the baby of the young man who was the Betterwear agent for our area. He called at our house selling household products and he and his wife lived in Burghead. We went to see the new baby and I gave them the embroidered bib, receiving sweets in return. I also used to embroider tray cloths with French knots and lazy daisy stitches but I can't recall that we actually used tray cloths in our house.

I had more success, eventually, with knitting. I could turn a heel on four needles and knit proper gloves with fingers. I made a pink scarf in garter stitch and Mum finished the ends with wool tassels made in different colours. I was pleased with it but stopped knitting after that, because it was too much of a struggle, until I was fifteen when I took it up again because I wanted a new jumper. Mum says that when she remembers the tears I shed learning to knit she is amazed at how much I have knitted since, even knitting Aran sweaters for a shop in Inverness in the 1970s.

On warm, sunny days the class would go on a nature ramble on the carse which was the name for the flat grassy area with drainage ditches next to Findhorn Bay, on the other side of the road from the school. Terns used to nest on a small island at the inner end of the bay but I think it was just an excuse for a walk as we didn't find very much except dead crabs. Rosie and I used to play there and in winter the tide would go out leaving a crust of ice which we used to jump on to break it. Just as well Mum didn't know what we were up to!

We had nature programmes for schoolchildren on the radio which always included a report from a faraway place called Tarn Hows. Many years later, I walked round Tarn Hows which is a small lake set in lovely scenery in the Lake District.

We had a singing programme on the radio and I liked one song called 'Marianina' which had a catchy tune. 'Marianina do not roam, whither whither is your home, come and turn us into foam.' After primary school I didn't hear Marianina again until I went on holiday to Austria and went to a concert where the tune was played. At school we learned other worthy songs like 'Men of Harlech', 'Rule Britannia' and 'Drink to me only with thine eyes,' which I thought was soppy. The songs taught to modern children are much more fun. In primary three I was selected to sing in front of the class because I had a good voice. This was the pinnacle of my singing career; it all went downhill after that.

We also had stories on the radio and the school was provided with books of pictures to accompany each story. The teacher would turn the pages as the story progressed. The one I remember was 'The Happy Prince' by Oscar Wilde, or at least it was an adaption for children of the original. It was a story about a statue of a little prince with ruby eyes and he was befriended by a swallow. In the end the swallow died and the statue was melted down. It was so sad my throat hurt and I cried.

The school had an annual sports day with sack races, three legged races, egg and spoon races and running races. The winner of each race was given three sweets, two for the second and one for the third. There was no mention of sweets rotting our teeth. One year we all went by coach to Burghead, a nearby seaside town and had our races there.

There was no thought of 'healthy eating' and were each given a small bottle of lemonade and a bag with two cakes which we ate in a hall. Rosie remembers being on a cold beach so it must have been too cold to eat outside even though it was in June.

When I was in my last year there, my class had a trip to Lossiemouth harbour and the fish market. It was supposed to be an educational trip but the smell was so awful that it made me feel sick and I had to retreat to the bus.

Everybody was encouraged to save money in the years after the war, including schoolchildren, and we had school bank books from the Trustee Savings Bank. We took a penny a week to school to add to our savings.

It seemed to take me a long time to learn to read, but eventually it all clicked into place I became a keen reader. Reading about Rupert the Bear in the Daily Express helped and it was there that I first saw the word 'cutlery'. It was either a misprint (my version) or my misreading but it became a family joke that knives and forks were called 'scutlery'.

Wooden boxes full of books were delivered to the school by the school library service and we were able to borrow them. I loved reading and always had my nose in a book. I still have a couple of Enid Blyton's 'Adventure' books which were birthday or Christmas presents. The children and their parrot Kiki in those books had such exciting lives! When I was ill in bed, Mum's friend lent me the full set of L. M. Montgomery's books, starting with 'Anne of Green Gables.' I also read the earlier books of the Chalet School series by Elinor Brent-Dyer, about a boarding school in Austria. They were all so much more interesting than our life at Kinloss.

We took exams at the end of each summer term and Rosie and I were almost always in the top three. Prize giving day was a big event in the school year and we always had new, matching dresses made by Mum. Sometimes I had my hair done too; Mum would wrap it in strips of rag overnight and next morning I had ringlets. I longed for curly hair!

Prize giving day 1956

We received prizes of books which were usually quite dull. None were by Enid Blyton; they were probably considered too frivolous and the only prize book I enjoyed reading was 'Black Beauty' by Anna Sewell which moved me to tears.

I can't say I enjoyed my primary school years because I was always scared of the teachers. Although I was a good child, I seemed to live in permanent fear of being slapped, or being thrashed on the hand with a leather belt called 'the strap', or seeing other children being strapped. Every teacher had one in his or her desk drawer and they were used for the most trivial misdemeanours. For example, one day we were told not to talk. Then the girl next to me (Pauline Lampart, it was you!) spoke to me and I reminded her we'd been told not to talk. The teacher heard me, hauled me out to the front of the

In my school outfit, with Judy the spaniel, 1951

class and I had to hold my hand out and was hit with the strap. I would have been about eight at the time. Well, that teacher got her comeuppance because one day she strapped one boy so badly that he still had red marks on his hands when he got home. His mother was livid and took him to the doctor in Forres, who happened to be the teacher's husband. Another teacher slapped me for being slow and I used to be in tears in the mornings, not wanting to go to school. In the end my mother went to the school and told the woman to leave me alone. It wasn't until I was grown up that Mum told me that my teacher had become pregnant by an RAF officer and had an abortion, which was illegal then.

I survived primary school and became dux in my last year.

Mr. Slorach, my teacher in primary six and seven, came to our house on a Saturday morning and told Mum that I was dux. I was photographed for the local paper and I still have my dux medal which was presented to me by the Group Captain's wife. I had to present her with a bouquet at the prize giving that year. Rosie was also dux in her last year.

*****

11 ENID BLYTON AND WHISKY GALORE

I saw my first ever film in the cinema at Forres. Rosie had been invited to a birthday party and I was peeved because I wasn't going too, so I was taken to see 'Bambi', the Walt Disney cartoon. I thought the seats were very uncomfortable, until Mum realised I hadn't folded the seat down before I sat on it. There was an RAF cinema at Kinloss which put on two films for children on Saturday mornings. We watched cowboys and Indians, Laurel and Hardy and a lot of films made especially for children such as 'It's Great To Be Young' about a school orchestra. Sometimes Mum took us to the 'first house' in the evening, if there was something suitable for children to watch, like 'Whisky Galore', a comedy about the SS Politician which was wrecked on a Scottish island with a cargo of whisky. The locals, deprived of whisky during the war, helped themselves to the bottles and found ways of hiding it from the 'authorities'.

When we were stuck for something to do, we used to pass the time by sitting on a gate by the main road writing the numbers of passing cars in a notebook. There weren't many cars around in those days so collecting numbers was a slow process. With hindsight, it was a waste of time but kept us occupied and out in the fresh air.

We had games such as ludo, snakes and ladders and draughts which Rosie always seemed to win as she was smarter than me. One day I was sure she was cheating at draughts so I picked up the board and banged her over the head with it. The draughts flew all over the place but oh,I felt better!

At home, Rosie and I read 'Enid Blyton's Magazine' each week and as well as stories the magazine had clubs in aid of charities like the Sunshine Homes for blind children and the Busy Bees in aid of the People's Dispensary for Sick Animals, which I joined because even then I had an interest in animals. One year I was given the 'Enid Blyton's Magazine' diary and in it was printed the name of the famous railway station in Wales, the one with the long name. I learned to spell it and I can still reel it off after all these years. That was also where I learned the alphabet of hand signs for the deaf. Modern educationalists look down at Enid Blyton but in post war Britain she encouraged people like me to read and brightened up our lives.

I read comics called 'Topper' and 'Beezer' then progressed to girls' comics when they became available. I read 'Girls Crystal' which had stories of boarding schools, always the best bits though, none of the loneliness and homesickness, but I thought at the time that boarding school had to be better than Kinloss Primary.

At Granny's house I read 'The Weekly News' which had a cartoon story about a sheepdog called Black Bob and 'People's Friend', a women's magazine with short stories. Mum had more interesting magazines, 'Woman' and 'Woman's Own', full of stories, recipes, knitting patterns and best of all, a page where women wrote in with their problems. Evelyn Home gave advice in 'Woman' and was a famous agony aunt for thirty six years. They also serialised books and one I have never forgotten is 'Seal Morning' by Rowena Farre, about a woman with a 'tame' wild seal in the north of Scotland.

There was an advertisement in those magazines for central heating which depicted a woman standing at the window of a warm house looking out on the frost and snow and my greatest desire was to live in a house with central heating. Well, that's one ambition I achieved!

Every Sunday, Dad bought the 'Sunday Post', 'Sunday Pictorial' and 'News of the World'.

I liked the Post best because it had good cartoon strips. 'Oor Wullie' was a little boy who sat on an upturned bucket and got into mischief with his friends Fat Bob, Soapy Soutar and Wee Eck. The Broons were a family who lived in a tenement in fictional Auchentogle, a Scottish industrial town. There was Maw and Paw, lanky Henry, ladies' man Joe, plain Daphne, glamorous Maggie, clever Horace, cheeky twin boys and 'the bairn' (we never knew her name) who was about four and wise beyond her years. Nearby lived Granpaw Broon and the stories revolved round their lives in the tenement and their thatched country cottage, the 'but and ben'. Both still have Christmas annuals and I read them well into adulthood.

We used to amuse ourselves with a little riddle about St Ives. "As I was going to St Ives, I met a man with seven wives. Every wife had seven sacks and in every sack were seven cats. Every cat had seven kittens. How many were going to St Ives?" The answer was one, because I was going to St Ives, so all the others were *coming* from St Ives!

Dad taught us how to play card games and we played Happy Families then graduated to knock-out whist and cribbage. That required a crib board with pegs to mark the score and also some mental arithmetic ability. I was hopeless but Rosie played well. Dad still has the crib board and scrawled on the back are the words 'Cribbage is a load of rubbish', written by me in a hissy fit. I must have come last again.

Besides reading, we used to play the piano and make scrap books, with pictures cut from magazines stuck down with flour and water paste. We used to collect lollipop sticks, put them into a pile and using one stick, try to dislodge one on the pile without moving others. Eventually we learned to ride bicycles and as Mum and Dad had a bike each we cycled on them when were tall enough to reach the pedals. Kinloss had a NAAFI shop on the camp and I would be sent on Mum's bike to buy groceries. I hated going because I worried that I couldn't find the shop, or worse, be unable to find my way home as all RAF buildings looked the same. I sometimes cycled on Dad's RAF bike and once I fell off and the serrated metal pedal made a deep cut in my leg. I had the scar for years.

As I got older, I discovered Radio Luxembourg. The reception was dreadful but I listened to pop music, so much more fun than songs learnt at school like the awful 'Drink to me only with thine eyes'. The whistling and crackling spoilt the reception but I put up with it. One song popular at the time was 'The Unchained Melody' which I thought even then was sentimental drivel. About this time I wrote to Tommy Steel, who was a popular pop singer at the time, to ask for his autograph, which I still have. I'm embarrassed to admit that I also had a bracelet with photos of him on it.

At 4pm on weekday afternoons, when I returned home from school, Mum always listened to a radio programme called 'Mrs. Dale's Diary' about a doctor's wife and her family. Her husband was Jim and her mother-in-law was Mrs. Freeman who owned a cat called Captain. Mrs. Morgan was the daily help, Monument was the gardener and she had a neighbour called Mrs. Mountford. I can't remember what they all did but the names have stuck in my mind.

Our family's favourite programme was 'Journey into Space', science fiction stories about space travel long before space ships and manned space flights. 'Jet' Morgan was the captain and his crew were called Doc, Mitch and Lemmy. In one story,

With Aunty Eileen on windy Findhorn Beach

they slept in beds which turned hard when it was time to get up and they also went to Bondi Beach, the first time I had heard of it. One evening we were driving home from Granny's house when the car broke down and we were so anxious to be home in time for 'Journey into Space' that we all got out and pushed until it started. We used to listen to comedy shows like 'Ray's a Laugh' with comedian Ted Ray and 'Life with the Lyons' with Ben Lyon and Bebe Daniels. 'Take it from here' was another popular programme with Jimmy Edwards and he had a little comedy sketch featuring the Glums, a couple called Ron and Eth. Eth whined a lot. We were entertained by radio serials before TV arrived and I remember listening in horror to 'Lord of the Flies' by William Golding. It was a story about schoolboys who were in a plane which crashed on an island and they ran wild because there were no adults to control them.

We would sometimes go to Findhorn, which has a lovely beach, to paddle on hot days. On the other side of the bay from Kinloss was the Culbin Sands, sand dunes planted with marram grass and fir trees to keep the sand stable. There was a myth that there was a village under the sand, buried in a storm long ago, but research has found that there were five farms under cultivation but no village. The storm which finished the farms was in 1694 and since then there have been stories of further storms revealing the chimneys of a big house, a chapel and a dovecote. We were told that the last wolf in Scotland was killed near Findhorn in 1743.

*****

12 LOCHINDORB AND WORKSOP

Sometimes on Saturday afternoons Mum would go shopping, taking the bus to Elgin about ten miles away and if it was fine Dad would take us out in the car for the afternoon. We would make a flask of tea and chunky sandwiches which we called 'cheese doorsteps'. Bread didn't come thinly sliced and packed in plastic bags; thick slices were cut off a loaf called a 'high pan' with a breadknife and to this day that's how bread is cut in Mum and Dad's house.

We'd drive off in the Morris 8, over the Dava Moor to Lochindorb, a bleak and lonely place along a one-track road. The loch has a little island with a ruined castle which reputedly has a dungeon beneath it with water in the bottom. Long ago, people would be thrown into it and left there. This was probably in the days of the Wolf of Badenoch, Alexander Stuart the Earl of Buchan who owned the castle. He was the third son of King Robert II of Scotland and is infamous for destroying Forres and Elgin, burning down Elgin Cathedral in 1390. He died in 1405 so the castle has a long history. It was probably too cold to paddle in the loch but we skimmed stones across the water then we sat and ate our sandwiches and drank the tea. It passed the afternoon.

Dad's mother, known as Granny-in-England, was widowed in 1918 when my grandfather was killed in the First World War. An ammunition dump exploded and he died of his wounds. She and her four children went to live with her sister, Great Aunt Mary, at 56 Mansfield Road, Worksop. We went in the Morris 8 from Kinloss to Worksop stay with Auntie Eileen, having picnics by the side of the road and staying in a hotel overnight because it was such a long journey. It was important to Dad to have a hotel with a lock up garage and one in Ecchelfechan had been selected. We had dinner in the hotel dining room and it was silver service. Rosie and I were very impressed because this was a totally new experience; I don't think we had ever eaten out before. That night we slept in a twin bedded room with a crack across the plaster in the ceiling and I lay awake looking at the crack, frightened that the ceiling was going to fall on top of me.

With Mum and Dad at Worksop

We went to what was reputedly Robert the Bruce's cave, one of several in Scotland and Ireland, which was on a cliff face at Kirkpatrick Fleming. We had to go along a wooden walkway above a steep drop to reach it and a man told us that it was where Bruce, who had suffered so many defeats he was about to give up and flee, had watched a spider trying again and again to make a web. According to legend he thought, 'If at first you don't succeed, try and try again' so he decided not to give up and continue on his quest. He won the Battle of Bannockburn in 1314 but in the end it was all in vain.

We stayed with my Auntie Eileen, Dad's only sister, and Uncle Reg who lived at 248 Mansfield Road. Uncle Reg had at one time been a bus driver and one day he took a bus out on a training trip and jammed it under a bridge. They had a dog called Bess and small, suburban garden with a little pond and a large clump of pampas grass. Rosie and I must have been bored so we picked the white fronds of the pampas grass and stuck them into a pair of topiary bushes bordering the path. I don't know if we were given a telling-off but the story still crops up from time to time.

Auntie Eileen had a cuckoo clock which used to fascinate us when the bird popped out. She also had a wonderful old fashioned wind-up gramophone and we always asked to hear a record called 'Sleigh Bells'. We had to wait until 1957 before we owned record player, a simple turntable which played through the radio.

We had an outing to the giant oak tree in the Sherwood Forest called Major Oak which is thought to be about a thousand years old and has been propped up with poles since Victorian times. It is hollow and we stood inside the tree trunk which was enormous I have been back to see the tree recently and it is now fenced off so you can no longer stand inside it and the huge branches are propped up with even more poles.

It must have been on this trip that we stopped at Edinburgh on the way home and visited Holyrood Palace. I can recall us being in a room with a man who was a guide and he told us that the red stain on the floor was David Rizzio's blood from when he was murdered in front of Mary Queen of Scots in 1566. I thought, 'Don't be silly!' I have been back to Holyrood recently and I see there is still a bloodstain by the window where he was killed, even though the floor was replaced in Victorian times.

*****

13 THE CORONATION AND THE STORM

On February 6th 1952 we were solemnly told at school that King George VI had died. Soon there was growing excitement because there was going to be a Coronation. It became even more exciting for me when I discovered that Coronation Day was to be June 2nd 1953, my ninth birthday, and we would have a day off school. For months before the big day, magazines were full of photographs of Princess Elizabeth and the Royal Family and I cut them out and collected them in a scrapbook. Then, after the event, I made another scrapbook of the ceremony itself. I still have both of them. At school we were each given a Coronation medallion in a box. I rushed home at lunchtime and persuaded Dad to drill a hole in my medal and Mum gave me a ribbon to thread through the hole, so I returned to school with my souvenir hanging round my neck. I regret it now as these things are collectable and mine is long gone. The day came and it was cold and wet. We sat by the radio, listening for hours to the build up, then the service itself. It was a huge event and it would have been better to see it on TV but there was none in the north of Scotland in those days. Later, a film about the Coronation called 'A Queen is Crowned' came to the RAF cinema and we all walked there from the school to see it.

Life takes strange twists. For the last twelve years I have worked as a guide at Mellerstain House, the childhood home of Lady Mary Russell, who was one of the Queen's attendants that day.

Across the road from the married quarters was Kinloss Abbey and next to it was a farm. An old farmer and his son lived there and they had a housekeeper called Mrs. McLennan. Mum bought fresh eggs from her and she always invited us in for a cup of tea. The farmhouse smelled of unwashed dogs and I didn't like it but Mrs. McLennan was generous with her tea and biscuits. We sometimes walked round the graveyard of the old abbey and it was there that I had an accident. I was running across the long grass and tripped over stone edging which surrounded a grave. I fell on to the other side of the edging, cutting my mouth badly. I was taken to Leanchoil Hospital in Forres but whatever happened when I got there has gone from my memory. However, there were no long lasting effects. My teeth survived.

During our time at Kinloss, we had all the common childhood illnesses like mumps, measles, German measles (rubella) and chicken pox. Rosie was very ill with measles and had to have the bedroom curtains closed to protect her eyes but generally speaking, apart from minor accidents and scraped knees, we were healthy children.

On the 31st January 1953, a combination of a high spring tide and a European wind storm caused severe flooding all the way down the east coast and a great many people were killed in south east England. The stream which flowed through Kinloss to Findhorn Bay literally became a sea of water. Gales and high tides brought the sea right up to Kinloss and the grounds of Kinloss House, a mansion which was empty at the time, were covered in water. Mum's friend, an old lady called Mrs. Duncan, lived in the lodge of Kinloss House and her home was flooded with stinking water. We often visited Mrs. Duncan who used to give us large, pale yellow biscuits called butter biscuits, spread with butter and syrup. The biscuits were not sweet and I loved them.

It was Mrs. Duncan who gave us our cat, Whisky. She was a lovely tortoiseshell kitten and Rosie and I gave her to Dad for his birthday, carrying her home from Mrs. Duncan's house in a shopping bag which we unzipped from time to time to look at her. She became very much Dad's cat. The kitchen unit was where we kept scarves and gloves, in the large bottom drawer. One day Mum opened the drawer and there was Whisky, fast asleep. Nobody even noticed she was missing.

One afternoon, I had come home from school and was sitting reading. It was a sunny afternoon and Whisky was sitting on top of an armchair by the window, snoozing in the sun. Mum was sitting waiting for the kettle to boil to make us a cup of tea when suddenly she saw an arm and hand holding an envelope come out from the side of the chair that Whisky was sitting on. The arm waved the envelope a couple of times then disappeared. Whisky leapt to her feet, her back arched and her tail in the air, her hair standing on end, looking down to the side of the chair to see what was going on. Then she jumped down and ran out of the room. I missed the whole incident!

We had a piano which Mum played and Rosie and I were sent to lessons with Miss Singer in Forres, travelling on the bus by ourselves. I never did get the hang of reading music but Rosie did well and passed her first exam, playing 'In an English Country Garden'. When we left for Kinloss for Singapore in 1957, the piano was sold and there were no more lessons.

Whisky had two or three lots of kittens. One night Mum heard the piano being tinkled so she crept downstairs, wondering if it was the ghost, to find a kitten walking up and down the piano keys. Eventually, when we went to Singapore, Whisky had to go to live with my granny at Birnie.

For a short time we also had a small tortoise called Napoleon, which cost two shillings and six pence from a pet shop in Elgin. We were ignorant about keeping tortoises and when he, or it could have been a she, hibernated we put him in a box near the coke stove and of course he died.

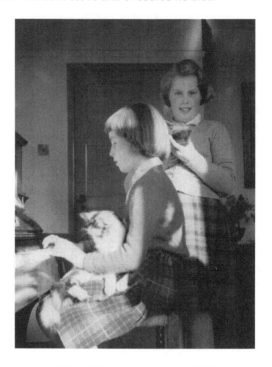

With Whisky at the piano 1954

It would have been that same bitterly cold winter when Mum heard about electric blankets so she went to Forres, our nearest town two miles away, and bought a double one. She was so pleased with it that she went back to Forres the next day and bought two single ones for Rosie and me. That house was cold, with none of the insulation of modern houses and we used to dress for school in the kitchen with Mum holding our clothes in front of a little electric fire to warm them before we put them on. We used to wake up to Jack Frost patterns inside the windows. We sat round the coal fire in the sitting room in the evenings, perhaps listening to the radio or reading, dreading having to venture into the cold hall and staircase to go upstairs to the toilet or to bed!

On winter nights in the north of Scotland we often saw the northern lights, the aurora borealis. Lights flickering in the sky were something we took for granted and we saw clear starry skies because there was no light pollution.

Mum was a very good seamstress. She had attended Elgin Technical College and then she was employed in Stronachs of Elgin's shop as a tailoress and dressmaker. After three years there she was called up to the WAAFs during the war. She had an electric Singer sewing machine which sat in a corner of the sitting room and she soon had a dressmaking business up and running. Officers' wives and ladies who were local gentry wore long ball gowns to go to formal parties in those days and Mum could make them to measure, as well as other clothes. She also did repairs and alterations.

One night, she was sitting sewing when the door opened and a woman in old fashioned clothes walked across the room and out through the other door to the hall. Mum says she wasn't an apparition, she looked like a solid person. She has no explanation; the house was new and built in a field so there had been nothing there previously. A lady called Joan used to help Mum with her sewing in the evenings. The curtains were never closed because there was just a field behind and nobody would be looking in but one night Joan saw somebody outside the window. Mum told her it was the ghost and that the back door would open, then the hall door and footsteps would go up the stairs. That's exactly what happened and Mum had to walk a very frightened Joan home!

With Mum 1948

During the war, Joan worked on a manual telephone exchange in Inverness. It was possible to listen in to conversations, including those of the Royal Family. She told us that she used to hear the Queen Mother inviting friends to 'dinsy winsy' We thought this was very funny as we called our mid-day meal 'dinner' and we had never heard of 'dinsy winsy'.

I think we were the only family with a car parked outside our house, the Morris 8, which was usually covered with a silver creation made by Mum. To protect it from the weather, she made a cover from a barrage balloon and lined it with blankets. It was a cosseted car!

There used to be a constant stream of other cars calling at our house. Our next door neighbour had been talking to a woman along the road who didn't know that Mum had a dressmaking business and that these visiting cars were customers and she said to our neighbour, 'Tell me, what's it like living next door to nobility?' We all had a good laugh at that. One titled lady used to arrive on her horse but I didn't hear what the neighbour had to say about that.

Mum was friendly with a woman who lost a baby to cot death. Probably because of a shortage of money it was Mum, who would have been about thirty at the time, who laid out the baby. She dressed it for burial in the petticoat of our lace christening robe. This was done in our house but I knew nothing about until many years later. When the bereaved parents left Kinloss, Mum planted flowers on the grave at Kinloss Abbey and took photos to send to the baby's parents.

Tinkers, as everybody called travelling people in those days, used to call at the house selling wooden clothes pegs. One cold day a woman who looked very poor and carrying a baby came to the door and Mum took pity on her and asked her in. The woman sat by the fire and fed her baby while Mum made her a cup of tea and gave her something to eat.

When knitting machines became available Mum bought a model called Rapidex and she used it to knit all our socks, jumpers and cardigans. She also gave talks and demonstrations for Rapidex to the local branches of the Scottish Women's Rural Institute. It was an amazing gadget at the time, but primitive compared with today's machines.

When a shop opened at Kinloss cottages, we discovered sweets. Up until then, Mum had enough sugar to make tablet (a sort of sugary, hard fudge) or toffee, which Rosie was allowed to make. She used to sit on the worktop stirring the hot mixture because she made the best toffee. After 1953 we had shop-bought sweets like gobstoppers, Spangles, Rowntrees fruit gums and sherbet dabs. At Easter, we used to have a chocolate egg full of sweets and we shared Mars bars, bigger than those we buy today, by chopping them up on the bread board. We also bought little tins of Creamola Foam, a powder which we added to water to make a fizzy, sweet drink. It contained eight ingredients including sugar *and* saccharin as well as flavourings and colour. We were given a Saturday sixpence, pocket money which would now be 2 ½ pence and I used to spend mine at the shop. Rosie hoarded hers and Granny used to say that money burnt a hole in my pocket because I used to spend my money so quickly.

Rosie put all her pocket money into a wooden moneybox which sat on the sitting room windowsill. Mum paid her a halfpenny each time she watered the pot plants and she would write this down in a little notebook and claim it with her Saturday sixpence. She saved her money for the fun fair which came to Forres each year. I had spent all my money by then but was given some to spend at the fair. At one stall we threw ping pong balls into fishbowls on a table and won a fish every time the ball landed in a bowl. Eventually we had seven little plastic bags with a fish in each and Mum and Dad had to buy a big fish tank. It sat on the dining room side table and Whisky used to walk round it, watching the fish.

We used to eat pink candy floss at the fair. One attraction was a woman who took her clothes off; nothing as seedy as a stripper because Mum took me in to watch. All I remember of the performance was the grand finale, when she modestly covered herself with a Davy Crockett hat. I was underwhelmed. The song which I associate with Forres fun fair is 'Hot Diggity'. It was a hit for Perry Como and must have been played loudly at the fair, 'Hot diggity, dog ziggity, boom what you do to me, it's so new to me, what you do to me.' Ah, they don't write songs like that now.

Kinloss House was an old mansion house with stables, lodges and a walled garden. When we lived at Kinloss it was empty and I know nothing of its history but Mum's friend Mrs. Duncan lived in one of the lodges and there was a gardener in the other lodge. He ran a market garden, growing fruit, vegetables and flowers for sale, all grown in the old walled garden. Mum was a regular customer and we were often sent round to buy vegetables and flowers which would have been organic but there was no such word then.

There were horses in the old stables, kept by a girl who hired them out for riding. On a very few occasions we were allowed to have five shillings (25p) for the two of us to have a half-hour ride round the grounds on Shetland ponies. Mine was called Smokey and Rosie's was a cantankerous beast called Wendy. Of course we had no fancy riding clothes and there were no safety hats but we enjoyed riding the ponies.

At the end of the row of old cottages in the village was Kinloss Church. Our family didn't attend church but, probably to give Mum some peace one Sunday morning, we were sent to Sunday school. Only once. We attended the church service first and I watched the organ being pumped manually, fearing that I might be asked to do it and I didn't know how. Then we went to Sunday School where we were split into groups. A girl who must have been all of fourteen, with pigtails and wearing a gabardine coat and a beret, took our class. She asked me a question which I didn't know the answer to because, to tell the truth, I didn't know *anything* about the Bible. Trying not to cry, I looked up at the ceiling and she said sarcastically, 'You won't find the answer on the ceiling!' Then I burst into tears and absolutely refused to go there ever again. That was the end of Sunday School for me. Later, I went there with the Girl Guides on Church Parades, one Guide carrying a flag and the rest marching behind. It was all very military.

Mrs. Slorach, the headmaster's wife, formed the guide company about 1956 and Rosie and I joined. I had wanted to be a Brownie but I thought you had to have a uniform to join and as I didn't have one I didn't go. All the Girl Guides were beginners and none of us had uniforms at first, then I got a navy blue skirt, blue blouse, a navy beret with a badge, a tie which was a folded triangular bandage tied at the back of my neck with a reef knot and a leather belt with a lanyard and whistle. In the breast pocket of my blouse I had to carry an Elastoplast tin full of 'punk', which was a bit of dried gorse, so that I could use it to light a fire if everything else was wet. I don't think I ever needed to use it.

We had two patrols and I was appointed patrol leader, probably because I was taller than the others, of the Golden Plover patrol (my choice of name, I was a bird watcher even then!)

We met in the primary school dining hall and learned things like semaphore and Morse code, which I have never needed to use, as well as useful things such as first aid and how to use a public telephone. Until then I had never used one, as only well off people had phones. Sometimes we played Kim's Game where several items were put on a tray, you looked at them for a few minutes then the tray was covered and you had to remember as many of the items as possible. I think it was supposed to train your memory but it didn't work for me.

I passed my Tenderfoot test, which included the ten Guide laws learnt off by heart and the Guide promise, 'I promise that I will do my best to do my duty to God and the Queen, to help other people at all times and obey the Guide Law.' Then I was given a 'gold' trefoil badge to fasten to my tie and had to clean it every week with Brasso until it shone.

I passed my cookery badge, which involved making a casserole in Mrs. Slorach's kitchen, and my Second Class badge. By the time I left the Guides in 1957 I had a few more badges including First Aid, Writing and my First Class badge.

An inter-company competition was held at a big house called The Bield, near Elgin. It was campfire cooking and Kinloss entered two teams, one from each patrol. We did a lot of practising before we set off with our ingredients, which included a packet of 'instant' chicken noodle soup which was new to the shops. We got our fire going in the beech woods round The Bield and cooked the soup along with flour and water dough rolled round a stick then cooked over the fire. It was more palatable if you added jam to the hole in the dough where the stick had been. Yes, we were not very sophisticated and easily amused in those days! Rosie's patrol won so we were very pleased. She and another guide also won the Moray County Tenderfoot Shield, a competition which was held on Cluny Hill in Forres.

In the spring of 1957 we had a weekend camping in a little pine wood opposite the school. We set up the Scouts' bell tent (Mr. Slorach was the Scoutmaster) and made a fire but I can't remember anything else, except that it was cold and hard sleeping on the ground. We all look quite happy in a photo taken at the camp so it must have been fine.

Guide camp. Rosie is second from left and I'm the tall one at the back.

The Scouts went to a proper camp somewhere on the other side of Elgin and they vaguely suggested that we could visit them. We were to be taken by a girl of about seventeen who assisted Mrs. Slorach. She wore a Guide uniform and we called her Cadet. The Scouts went off to their camp and I hadn't forgotten about the invitation but for some reason Cadet could not, or would not, go. I rounded up a few Guides and Mum took us to the railway station and bought the tickets for us. We changed trains in Elgin and arrived at the Scout camp to find we weren't expected but it all worked out as we were fed, entertained and looked after then put back on the train. We changed at Elgin and on the train an elderly lady started talking to us. We chatted politely, as one did in those days, and just as well because she turned out to be a retired Guide Commissioner. She wrote to Mrs. Slorach and told her how well behaved we were and said she should be proud of us. I found out later that Cadet wasn't capable of taking us on two trains to the Scout camp, but I did it and I was only twelve or thirteen. Many years later, when I was married, I was in a restaurant near Nairn and I recognised Mr. and Mrs. Slorach at a nearby table. They invited me and my husband and children to their house in Forres, where they had moved after retirement, and we had a long chat about the old days at Kinloss.

*****

14 AUNTY EILEEN

We liked Aunty Eileen. She used to visit us with her husband, Uncle Reg, driving up to Kinloss from their home in Worksop to stay with us in the summer. Rosie and I used to look forward to their visit as it was a change to have someone to stay. Aunty Eileen always wore a beige dress with a pattern of playing cards on it. When she felt unwell, she used to say she was 'poorly'. Another word from Worksop was 'dollyflops'. If you are sitting doing nothing, you are dollyflopsing. It's a word I still use and that's where it came from.

She gave me her beautiful Edwardian doll with a china face and glass eyes with eyelashes. Her name was Hannah and Mum made her a dress from blue taffeta with little pink roses. One day, I took her to the back door to show her to a friend and on the way back I slipped on the dining room rug and Hannah fell to the floor, her lovely face smashed to pieces. I still haven't got over it.

In fact that wasn't the only disaster I had slipping on the dining room rug. Dad had made a bucketful of elderberry wine, adding a whole bottle of brandy and it had been left to mature in a corner. The floor was polished concrete and I slipped on the rug, hitting the bucket and the purple contents flew everywhere.

When I was fifteen and living at RAF Scampton, Aunty Eileen often came to see us from Worksop. One day, when everybody was outside and Eileen, Mum and I were in the sitting room, there was an unexpected noise, something trivial, but Mum said, 'It could be a ghost, like the one at Kinloss!' Then she told us about the strange things that used to happen there, but I wasn't surprised as I had seen the ghost. One night I saw a white figure standing in the bedroom doorway and I remember pulling the covers up over my face so that it couldn't see me. Later, when Mum looked in on us before going to bed, she saw me clutching the covers and guessed that I'd seen the ghost. I recall telling her about it the next day, though how I knew what a ghost was I can't remember, and she told me I'd seen *her*, not a ghost. I didn't believe her!

Another visitor to Kinloss was Simon, the lodger who lived at Granny's house. He sometimes went with Mum and Dad to the Families Club on a Saturday night, for a drink and to play tombola. (Many years later, tombola became Bingo.) Simon used to sleep on a mattress on the sitting room floor and one night the bedcovers were suddenly grabbed and pulled off. When he told Mum and Dad what happened, he said he'd never been so frightened in his life, even though he'd slept among dead Germans in the war.

Mum used to tell us about a frightening experience she had when she was in the WAAFs. She was cycling along a country road in the dark and realised she was being followed by a 'thing'. It turned out to be a barrage balloon which had broken free from its mooring and was bowling along the road behind her in the wind!

Mum and Dad often went to the Families Club on a Saturday night and we were left on our own, asleep. There was only a wooden door separating our upstairs landing from next door (so that the building could be two two-bedroomed houses or one with one bedroom and one with three-bedrooms) and the lady next door could hear us if we shouted. Bribed with a promise of some of Mum's tombola winnings, we were always good and never came to harm. Once a young airman came to babysit and as I was awake, he offered me a cup of cocoa. When I had finished, he offered me another so I said, 'Yes please', not because I wanted another but because I thought it would be impolite to refuse! He told Mum he'd spent the evening running up and down stairs with cups of cocoa. He never came again.

Rosie and I once went to the Families Club to see Punch and Judy, which we had to pay for, but the couple supposed to be putting it on had no Punch and Judy show so we played games and went home. It was all a waste of time and I remember being upset and disappointed. They said they would come again with Punch and Judy but they never did and that was my first experience of a con trick, which I suspect it was.

We spent most weekends and school holidays with Granny at Birnie, first going by bus then in the Morris. Sometimes we went on the pillion of Simon's motor bike which was the best way to travel! To get back to Kinloss by bus on Sunday evening involved a long walk from the village, past Birnie Kirk, to a place called the Cloddach where we waited on the main road for a bus with slatted, wooden seats which took us to Forres, then we caught another bus to Kinloss. Rosie and I carried our clothes packed in our schoolbags. We liked being at Birnie because there was much more to do. There wasn't even a wood to play in at Kinloss.

However, there was some entertainment. On Bonfire Nights, the RAF put on a big bonfire and fireworks display on the airfield and we used to go every year with Mum and Dad. As well as fireworks, the RAF used to get rid of their out of date Very lights (flares) which were as spectacular as the fireworks. They also gave us hot soup.

A Christmas party was also put on for us and we went dressed in our best frocks for games, food and a visit from Santa. One year I was given a box of Chinese Chequers. I already owned the game, which I didn't like, and cried with disappointment all the way home. Ungrateful little madam! I didn't stop to think that some children got nothing at all.

In June 1956, I finished at Kinloss Primary and expanded my horizons to Forres, the nearby town.

*****

15 *FORRES*

Forres was our nearest town. It has a beautiful park, Grant Park, and Cluny Hill is part of it. At the top of the hill is Nelson's Tower, built in 1806 in honour of Horatio Nelson. It is three storeys high and in our lunch hours we pupils at Forres Academy often went up to the top of the tower as there was a spectacular view of the surrounding countryside. It is still free to go in but now it is only open in the afternoons.

When I was in primary five at Kinloss we had a class outing to the tower. It was a sunny day in June 1954 and there was an eclipse of the sun. We were told not to look at it directly but we could look through a few black and white photograph negatives, which we did. We went to Forres by bus and climbed the tower to watch the eclipse.

At the edge of the park, next to the main road, is the witch's stone commemorating the time when witches were rolled down the hill in a spiked barrel. If the witch was still alive the barrel was set alight. This must have been before the hill was covered with trees. The stone marks where one barrel came to rest and it sits in a wall. It was a hedge in my day.

Sueno's Stone stands by the roadside just outside Forres on the road to Kinloss. It was an ancient stone covered in symbols and nothing much was known about it when I passed it on my way to Forres Academy but now it is protected in an armoured glass case. It is over twenty feet high and is thought to be from about AD900. Scenes of a battle and a Celtic cross are carved on it.

In my final year at primary school I took the eleven plus exam and went on to Forres Academy. I was twelve in June and started in August. There was no preparation for the next school as there is for children nowadays, not even a visit, and we just turned up on the first day of the autumn term. Children were graded by ability, classes A to E in first year and I was in class 1A, doing French, Latin and science as well as the basic subjects. It was tolerable but I didn't like gym, as PE was called, as I'm not sporty so I used to dread Tuesdays and Thursdays. What I hated most was having to play hockey in Grant Park, in view of anybody who wanted to sit and stare, in our green school bloomers. Everybody seemed to think it was acceptable to have young girls running round a public park in their knickers but nobody protested, except me. I was horrified. Now that I'm a mother and a granny, I think this practice was wrong and somebody should have put a stop to it. I had a pair of fashionable pleated shorts made by Mum, and I wore them.

I was only there for three terms, then we left Kinloss for Singapore.

Forres was where we went if we needed to visit the dentist. Having your teeth drilled was a painful process as drills weren't as refined as they are now and there was no anaesthetic. I once spent a hot, summer weekend in agony with toothache. All of one side of my head ached (neuralgia was mentioned) and I just had to suffer until the dentist saw me on the Monday. I remember the pain but not the treatment.

In our last summer at Kinloss we went for a day out to Oban. We packed food and drove all the way down Loch Ness, stopping for a roadside picnic. You could do that in those days as there was hardly any traffic and it was there that Rosie and

I scrambled up some rocks and saw an adder which reared up at us. The journey to Oban was a long drive in those days and when we got there we found that we could have a trip on a ferry. I can't recall where we went but it was late when we arrived back at Oban and we stopped on the way home to eat what was left of the picnic, bread and butter. Even if there had been anywhere open serving food, we wouldn't have gone in because we just didn't eat out in those days. I've made up for it since.

At Kinloss in 1956

Towards the end of 1956, Dad was told he was going to be posted to the Far East and left to fly out there early in 1957, to Kuala Lumpur in Malaya. Then, when I was staying at Granny's house, I became unwell and had to have the doctor, a lady from Elgin. She had no idea what was wrong and looking back nor do I, but I was in bed at Kinloss for a couple of weeks. That's when I read all the 'Anne of Green Gables' books. That delayed our programme of injections (tetanus and typhoid which made my arm stiff and ache for days, yellow fever which nipped and stung and a smallpox vaccination) to go abroad so it was the end of August before we set off by sea on the troopship SS Nevasa. I remember asking Mum if we had been told we were going to live at RAF Changi but at the time we hadn't been told where we were going. Eventually we heard that Dad had been posted to Kuala Lumpur in Malaya but I was certain that we were going to Changi. During the three weeks we were at sea we had no contact with Dad and when we arrived in Singapore he met us and told us that while we were on the ship he had been posted away from Kuala Lumpur. We were going to live at RAF Changi, which was our home for the next two years.

In the summer of 1957 I had become a teenager and left my childhood in Morayshire behind as I set off on a huge adventure, a new life and new friends on the other side of the world. But that's another story.

The houses in Tedder Road were demolished some time ago and RAF Kinloss was closed down in 2011, a victim of government cuts.

*****